Successful Farming —By Mail

Steve Kennedy

Calculated Industries, Inc.
2010 North Tustin • Orange • California • 92665

Author's Acknowledgements

I'd like to thank the entire staff at Calculated Industries — Bill, Marie, Gail, Carol, Tink, Jill, Lorraine, "Big" Bill, Dana, and Becky — for their help in producing this book. Special thanks also go out to Mark Paulsen, my assistant, and Ken and Fred Alexander, my publishers.

 Second Printing.

Publication Data

Kennedy, Steve C., 1957–
Successful farming by mail.

Includes index.

ISBN 0-944041-01-9

Printed in the United States of America

Table of Contents

Part III — Words That Make Money

Part IV — The Sales Letter

Part V — Mailing Your Mailings

To my wife, Mary Ellen,
whose love helped write
the pages that follow.

Part I

Farming for Profits

1. Introduction to Farming By Mail

All of us in the real estate profession are faced with the problem of having *too many* possible prospects. In the city of Pomona, where I live, there are over 110,000 people. And tens of thousands of them own real estate of some sort.

If I branch out into the entire county of Los Angeles, there are over 6 million people and more than a million property owners.

This "problem" leads many of us to a "hit-or-miss" approach to marketing our professional services.

Instead of focusing on a manageable segment of the market, we try to serve them all. The trouble is that, in trying to serve them all, we serve none of them very well.

What Is Farming?

In short, farming is the process of focusing your real estate marketing efforts on a select and manageable segment of the marketplace called, not surprisingly, a "listing farm" or "farm."

Basically there are two types of farms: (1) A

territorial farm and (2) a social farm. In Chapter 2 you will see the differences between the two types and how to select which one is right for you as well as its optimal size.

Three Ways to Cultivate Your Farm

There are endless ways to reach your farm, but the three most common are: (1) in person, (2) by phone, and (3) by mail. This can be called "the farm marketing mix."

All three are, of course, important and ideally will work together. An example of their working together

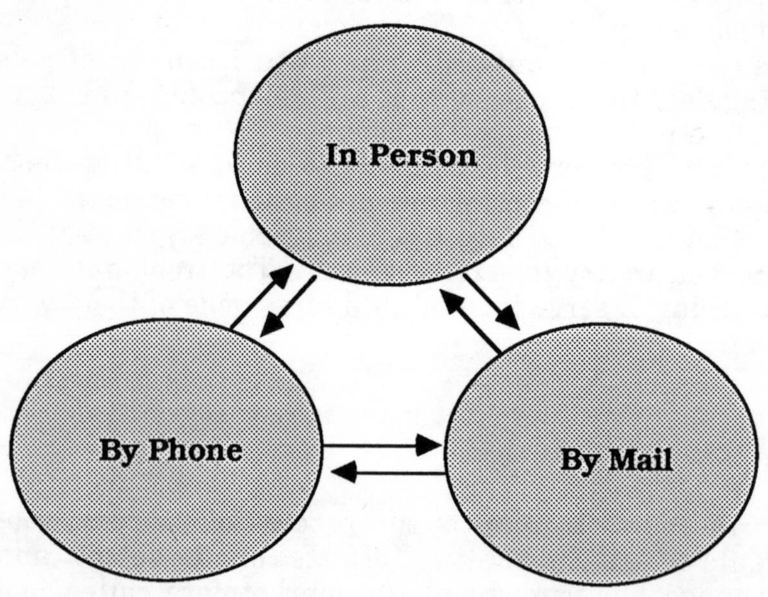

Reaching the Farm — The three main ways to reach your farm are: in person, by phone, and by mail. Ideally these three work together.

is this:

> *Agent Mary Williams sends out a monthly newsletter to her farm of approximately 300 homes. Enclosed in the envelope with the newsletter, she usually includes a return postcard for a Free Comparative Market Analysis.*
>
> *Last month one of her prospects returned the card by mail. Upon receiving it, she called the homeowner by phone to set up an in-person appointment for the evaluation.*
>
> *Less than a week later, she had the exclusive listing.*

As you can see from this example, all three elements working together brought the best results for Agent Mary Williams.

About This Book

This book is going to look primarily at the third element of this farm marketing mix — mail contact — and particularly the sales letter format used to generate prequalified leads.

However, it is important to note the way in which you must combine all the elements — mail, phone, and personal contact — to ensure the best results from your farm efforts.

So while you will focus on the mailing aspects of farming, you must always keep in mind how your proposed mailings will work with the other elements of this mix and, ultimately, toward your true goal of increased sales and listings.

If you are relatively new to farming and, in particular, farming by mail, this book should be ideal for you.

On the other hand, if you are already doing a lot of farming by mail, do not close the book just yet. Even though some of this may be review for you, hopefully there will be a few tips and tricks to save you money and help you better reach your prospects.

Steve C. Kennedy

Pomona, California
March 18, 1987

2. How to Select Your Real Estate Farm

The last chapter discussed the different types of farms and how to select yours. In this chapter you will look in depth at the farm selection process.

Two Types of Farms

Again, there are essentially two types of real estate farms: (1) territorial farms and (2) social (or club) farms.

Territorial Farms

A territorial farm is the most common in real estate. Typically it is a neighborhood, tract, or housing development that is tied together geographically.

The benefits of a territorial farm should be obvious. For one thing, it is easy to manage. You can drive through it and see what is happening, or walk the streets and meet many of your prospects at once.

Plus, it has the additional benefit of synergy — that is, as you start to become more visibly successful in your farm, things tend to snowball because neighbors talk and always notice "sold" signs!

Another benefit of a territorial farm is that research is usually easy to do. For example, when you first select a farm area, you can drive through it, see what other signs are out, and if there is already someone successfully tilling its soil. Further, you can easily study past sales activity.

Social Farms

While less common than territorial farms, social farms are often much more profitable.

A social farm is a group of prospects who belong to the same organization, such as a church group, club, association, or even a workplace.

The social farmer typically joins this organization and often becomes one of its most visible members.

The benefits of a social farm are less obvious. For one thing, it is a little more difficult to manage, because you cannot drive through it or walk the streets and see what is happening.

However, often you will have more than ample opportunity to meet with and get to know your farm in a social organization.

In addition, the same synergy found in a territorial farm is often more prevalent in a social farm, since the prospects usually know each other better and communicate more often. However, "sold" signs will most often go unnoticed.

But the biggest problem with a social farm is doing hands-on research. It is very difficult to study past sales activity, since your prospects are often spread out geographically — but it is possible.

More than likely you will have to work with general

information (such as that provided by your local board) for your farm research.

Second, you may not be the only real estate farmer in the organization. In fact, there may be several others.

However, there is the unseen benefit of a social farm — that is, you will probably have some fun doing it. And after all, there is more to life than sales, listings, and board meetings.

Which Type of Farm Is Right for You?

There is no right or wrong type of listing farm. But there are some questions you can ask yourself to decide which of these two types of farms you will feel more comfortable dealing with:

Are there any organizations you currently belong to which you could use as a social farm?

Are there any organizations you would like to join which you could use as a social farm?

Do you enjoy these "club" environments or would you rather work within a neighborhood?

Is the neighborhood you live in a farm prospect?

Are there good, well-segmented neighborhoods or tracts in your area that would make a good farm?

Other Farm Considerations

When selecting a farm area there are plenty of other factors to look at as well.

First, you need to feel comfortable with and relate to the residents or members of your farm. If you think golf is a stupid game, then it would be silly to use a men's or women's club at the local golf course for a social farm. By the same token, if you like Levi's, cowboy boots, and pickup trucks, then cruising the Mercedes-laden streets of Beverly Hills might not be your best territorial farm either.

Second, you need to look, if you can, at the income potential of your farm. This includes things like selling price and turnover ratios. These things are especially important when you are comparing prospective farms.

And finally, be sure to do some careful checking of the competition to make certain you are not butting heads against someone who has already got a firm foothold on the soil.

Sizing Up the Farm

One of the most common questions asked by new "farmers" is what size farm to maintain. This, of course, depends a lot on your abilities and ambitions, but hopefully the computations ahead and the accompanying worksheet will give you some insight.

Let Commissions Be Your Guide

For most people, the best method for sizing up a farm is based on your specific income goals and the commissions needed to reach them.

To begin, you must establish in your own mind a reasonable and attainable goal of how much money you want to generate *from your farm* in gross commissions. Remember, of course, you will still have other revenue sources outside of your farm.

To find out what size farm you need to attain your commission goal — which for this example we'll assume to be $60,000 per year — you will need to look at several ratios. So grab a pencil, some scratch paper, and your calculator.

The ratios to look at are:

1. *Average Gross Commission Percentage*
2. *Average Sales Price*
3. *Average Gross Commission Dollars*
4. *Annual Turnover Rate*
5. *Farm Penetration Percentage (estimated)*

Average Gross Commission Percentage — This one is a little tricky. It pertains to the number of homes on which you will split a commission (via co-op sales) versus the number of homes you sell on your own and for which you will keep the full commission.

For this ratio it is best to use your own past listing history. For example, say last year you had 40 listings, and of those, 30 were sold through cooperative multiple listings (50/50 split between the listing agent and selling agent), and the other 10 were sold outright. If 6% is the normal commission in your area, then that means you had an overall Average Gross Commission Percentage per listing as follows:

30 Listings x .03 (3%) Ea. = .90
10 Listings x .06 (6%) Ea. = <u>.60</u>
= 1.50 ÷ 40 Listings = .0375 (or 3.75%)

This means the Average Gross Commission on each of your listings was 3.75%.

Average Sales Price — This is fairly straightforward. You simply find the average sales price for homes sold in the prospective farm area. Add all of the sales prices together and divide by the number of homes sold. For simplicity, say those 40 homes sold for a total of $4,000,000.

$4,000,000 ÷ 40 Homes = $100,000 Average Sales Price

Average Gross Commission Dollars — Here you simply take the Gross Commission Percentage calculated above and multiply it by the Average Sales Price.

In this case, that is $100,000 x 3.75%, or $3,750, which means you will generate $3,750 in gross commission for each listing you get.

So with this calculated, you can now find the number of listings you need to obtain in order to reach your goal of $60,000 in gross commissions:

$60,000 ÷ $3,750 per Listing = 16 Listings Needed

Now that you have determined the number of listings required, you need just two more pieces of information: the area's Annual Turnover Rate and your Farm Penetration.

Annual Turnover Rate — This is the "formula" for determining the number of homes sold in any given year, typically the most recent year, in your prospective farm area. Or it can be calculated from your board or multiple listing service (MLS) information.

Basically the formula works like this: Divide the

total number of sales for the year by the size of the prospective farm.

# Homes Sold in Last 12 Months	88
÷ Total Size of Prospective Farm	÷ 720
Annual Turnover Rate	**12.22%**

So you know that for the example problem, you have an Annual Turnover Rate of 12.22%.

(To get a more accurate figure, it is often best to take a couple of years' worth of information. If you do this, make sure use the *yearly average* for your calculation.)

If you divide the number of listings needed to meet the income goal (from above) by the Annual Turnover Rate, you get the total farm size. This assumes that you got *all* of the listings in the farm.

16 Listings ÷ 12.22% Turnover Rate = 130.93 (or 131) Homes

But you are not quite finished yet. Nobody gets all of the listings in a farm area — even the best farmers get nudged out by relatives, etc.

That is where the final ratio, Farm Penetration, comes into play.

Farm Penetration — This is the percentage of total homes listed in the farm area on which you will get the listing. Obviously this will vary — 50% is very good, and 60% to 75% is excellent.

Just starting out, you cannot expect to harvest the same results as if you had been working at it for awhile. Moreover, it is going to take time, usually 6 to 18 months, just to get it started. *Rome wasn't built in a day!*

For the example here (one in which you are starting a brand new farm) use 40% Farm Penetration.

Now that you have estimated the Farm Penetration, all you need to do is divide the number of homes needed, if you got *all* the listings in the farm, by the Farm Penetration to get your necessary farm size.

131 Homes ÷ 40% Penetration = 327.50 (or 328) Homes

At last, you have done it!

Summarizing, in order to achieve gross commissions of $60,000 from your farm, you must have a farm size of 328 homes. This is based on an Average Sales Price of $100,000, a 12.22% Turnover Rate, your ability to get 40% of the listings in the farm (40% Farm Penetration), and your ability to sell one fourth of the farm listings outright and the other three fourths through your co-op multiple listing service.

The completed "Prospective Farm Size" worksheet on the next page, and the blank one on the two pages that follow, are designed to help you determine your optimal farm size based on your own income goals.

Prospective Farm Size — Example

Your Annual Commission Goal $60,000

1. **Average Gross Comm. Percentage**
   - #30 Co-Op Listings x 3 % = .90
   - #10 Solo Listings x 6 % = .60

   Sum 40 Total % = 1.50

   Divide Total % by # of listings ÷ 40

   Average Gross Commision % = 3.75%

2. **Average Sales Price**
   - Add up all sales prices for farm area and div. by the # of homes sold = $100,000

3. **Average Gross Comm. Dollars**
   - Multiply Avg. Sale Price (#2) $100,000
     by Avg. Gross Comm. % (#1) x 3.75%

     Avg. Gross Comm. Dollars = $ 3,750

4. **Number of Listings Needed**
   - Divide Annual Comm. Goal 60,000
     by Avg. Comm. Dollars (#3) ÷ $3,750

     Number of Listings Needed = 16

5. **Annual Turnover Rate**
   - Divide number of sales for year 88
     by total number of homes in prospective farm (or MLS) area ÷ 720

     Annual Turnover Rate = 12.22%

6. **Farm Size If You Got 100% of Listings**
   - Divide Number of Listings (#4) 16
     by Ann. Turnover Rate (#5) ÷ 12.22%

     Farm Size at 100% of Listings = 131

7. **Farm Penetration**
   - Est. percentage of homes in the farm on which you'll get the listing = 40%

8. **Final Size of Farm Needed for Goal**
   - Divide Farm Size at 100% (#6) 131
     by Farm Penetration (#7) ÷ 40%

     Actual Size of Farm Needed = 328

Example of completed Prospective Farm Size sheet.

Sizing Up Your Farm

Prospective Farm #1

Your Annual Commission Goal $ ______

1. **Average Gross Comm. Percentage**
   - # ___ Co-Op Listings x ___% = ______
   - # ___ Solo Listings x ___% = ______

   Sum ____ Total % = ______
   Divide Total % by # of listings ÷ ______
   Average Gross Commision % = _____%
2. **Average Sales Price**
   - Add up all sales prices for farm area and divide by the # of homes sold = $____
3. **Average Gross Comm. Dollars**
   - Multiply Avg. Sale Price (#2) ______
     by Avg. Gross Comm. % (#1) x ______
     Avg. Gross Comm. Dollars = $____
4. **Number of Listings Needed**
   - Divide Annual Comm. Goal ______
     by Avg. Comm. Dollars (#3) ÷ ______
     Number of Listings Needed = ______

Prospective Farm #2

Your Annual Commision Goal $ ______

1. **Average Gross Comm. Percentage**
   - # ___ Co-Op Listings x ___% = ______
   - # ___ Solo Listings x ___% = ______

   Sum ____ Total % = ______
   Divide Total % by # of listings ÷ ______
   Average Gross Commision % = _____%
2. **Average Sales Price**
   - Add up all sales prices for farm area and divide by the # of homes sold = $____
3. **Average Gross Comm. Dollars**
   - Multiply Avg. Sale Price (#2) ______
     by Avg. Gross Comm. % (#1) x ______
     Avg. Gross Comm. Dollars = $____
4. **Number of Listings Needed**
   - Divide Annual Comm. Goal ______
     by Avg. Comm. Dollars (#3) ÷ ______
     Number of Listings Needed = ______

5. **Annual Turnover Rate**
   - Divide number of sales for year by total number of homes in prospective farm (or MLS) area ______ ÷ ______

   Annual Turnover Rate = ______%

6. **Farm Size If You Got 100% of Listings**
   - Divide Number of Listings (#4) ______ by Ann. Turnover Rate (#5) ÷ ______

   Farm Size at 100% of Listings = ______

7. **Farm Penetration**
   - Est. percentage of homes in the farm on which you'll get the listing = ______%

8. **Final Size of Farm Needed for Goal**
   - Divide Farm Size at 100% (#6) ______ by Farm Penetration (#7) ÷ ______

   Actual Size of Farm Needed = ______

5. **Annual Turnover Rate**
   - Divide number of sales for year by total number of homes in prospective farm (or MLS) area ______ ÷ ______

   Annual Turnover Rate = ______%

6. **Farm Size If You Got 100% of Listings**
   - Divide Number of Listings (#4) ______ by Ann. Turnover Rate (#5) ÷ ______

   Farm Size at 100% of Listings = ______

7. **Farm Penetration**
   - Est. percentage of homes in the farm on which you'll get the listing = ______%

8. **Final Size of Farm Needed for Goal**
   - Divide Farm Size at 100% (#6) ______ by Farm Penetration (#7) ÷ ______

   Actual Size of Farm Needed = ______

This form is designed to help you determine the size of your farm or to compare a couple of farms.

Other Factors to Consider in Sizing Your Farm

While it is important to let your income goals guide you in your farm size selection, there are other factors to consider.

First, there is manageability. Will you be able to serve the farm in person, on the phone, and through the mail? If your farm has 1,000 homes in it, you might be able to serve them by mail easily enough; but in order to personally see each homeowner twice a year, you would need to see an average of eight homeowners each and every working day (based on five workdays a week for 50 weeks per year).

That is quite a bit!

On the other hand, if you do mailings to your farm, the US Postal Service grants a fairly significant discount on postage costs when you mail to 200 or more homes — the minimum number required to mail by bulk rate.

And this discount (as you will see later) can amount to quite a savings — from 43% to 54% depending on the size of your farm.

Finally, keep your income goals reasonable and attainable. Your farm will not be your only source of income, but hopefully it will be a major one.

Summary

In this chapter you looked at the basics of farming and how to select and size your prospective farm. While some of the mathematics were perhaps a bit complicated — yet hopefully simplified by the included worksheets — they are necessary to get a good start on your farming efforts.

From here forward, this book devotes most of its attention to the specific topic of *farming by mail.*

3. Getting Started Farming By Mail

There is money in the mail!

That does not mean the envelope with Ed McMahon's smiling face proclaiming that "You may have already won $10 million!"

Instead, it refers to the business end of direct mail and, more specifically, how you as a real estate professional can use it to cultivate your farm area.

What Is Direct Mail?

Before getting started on the applications of direct mail for real estate, it is important to get a little background on what direct mail is and how it works.

The definitions of direct mail are wide-ranging. Once a term reserved for itself, today it is considered a part of the broad-based term, "direct marketing."

And the accepted definition of that, as created by the Direct Marketing Association (DMA), is:

Direct Marketing — The total activities by which products and services are offered to market segments in one or more media for informational purposes, or to solicit a direct response from a present or prospective customer or contributor by mail, telephone or other access.

Why Direct Mail Is Growing

According to *Direct Marketing* magazine, gross mail order sales in 1986 topped $133 billion, and that figure continues to grow at a rate of about 15% per year.

Moreover, the US Postal Service reported that in the first quarter of 1987, third-class mail (the most common type used by direct marketers) accounted for 38.6% of all domestic mail.

This, too, is growing.

Several factors account for this tremendous growth, not the least of which is the high cost of other selling methods, especially personal selling.

McGraw-Hill research indicates that a single in-person sales call costs over $220. That is why methods such as direct mail and telemarketing — or often a combination of both — have become such popular ways to qualify prospects economically.

Other factors also help account for the growth of direct mail in recent years. These include social changes, such as increased educational levels and the vast number of working women.

Technology has also played a role, as computers are now able to select and segment markets more profitably, as well as maintain customer files quickly and simply.

What Can Be Sold by Mail?

Almost anything — *and everything* — has been sold by mail, from ant farms to pet rocks and zebra skin rugs. If someone is willing to buy it, someone else will be willing to sell it — by mail.

And firms that market by mail range from mom-and-pop kitchen-table operations all the way up to the multimillion dollar Sears catalog, with thousands and thousands of companies in between.

Furthermore, there are thousands of ways to market by mail.

But basically most of these methods can be broken down into two categories: one-step and two-step.

One-Step Direct Response

One-step direct response, as its name would suggest, goes for the actual sale in the initial ad or mail piece. A full-fledged offer or proposition is made, and the response is to either accept or reject the offer as presented.

Here are some examples of one-step direct-response offers:

Large Display Ads — You open your morning newspaper and find a full-page ad with a bold headline proclaiming, "Lose Weight While You Sleep With New Miracle Diet Pills." In addition to many lines of copy about what these "miracle" diet pills do, you find in the bottom right-hand corner an order form (as well as an "800" number for rush service) to purchase a 30-, 60-, or 90-day supply.

Direct Mail — You open your mail-box to find an envelope from *The Wall Street Journal.* Inside, you find a letter, order card, and postage-paid return envelope, all detailing your "special" subscription offer — 13 weeks for $29.75, money-back guarantee.

Catalogs — The Sharper Image® sends you a 64-page, full-color catalog with all the latest in electronic gizmos. Each of the items listed includes a price; and bound in the center is a detailed order form and return envelope.

Television — It is late at night, and you are watching cable TV when a 120-second commercial comes on for the "Greatest Soul Sounds of the 60s" — three records, two long-play cassettes, or two 8-track tapes for just $17.95. ("Avoid COD charges and use your Visa, MasterCard, or American Express. Call right now.")

All of these are examples of one-step direct-response offers. And, of course, there are many, many more.

Two-Step Direct Response

Two-step direct response works differently in that the initial offer presented is for some kind of nonbuying follow-up action — for example, to send for further information.

Here are some examples of two-step direct-response offers:

Classified Ads — In the back of every issue of *Realtor News®* you will find several newsletter companies promoting their services using small classified ads offering free information.

Television — Discount Broker Charles Schwab airs a television commercial offering free information on opening an account. Simply call an "800" number, and your kit will come by mail.

Direct Mail — A second letter in your mailbox comes from IBM. Since most people will not buy computers without seeing them, IBM's offer is for a free pocket-size calculator when you take the enclosed certificate to your authorized IBM dealer for a demonstration.

These are all examples of two-step direct response. Most of what you mail to your real estate farm is this type of marketing.

Why Direct Mail Works

Targets Your Message

More than any other marketing method, direct mail allows you to target your message.

Say, for example, you have just invented the world's first left-handed tennis racket. In order to market it, you need to reach two well-defined groups (one of which is part of the other): (1) tennis players and (2) tennis players who play left-handed.

Not an easy task through conventional marketing methods! Using such methods, it would be difficult to isolate your target market from the markets you do not need to reach, such as right-handed tennis players.

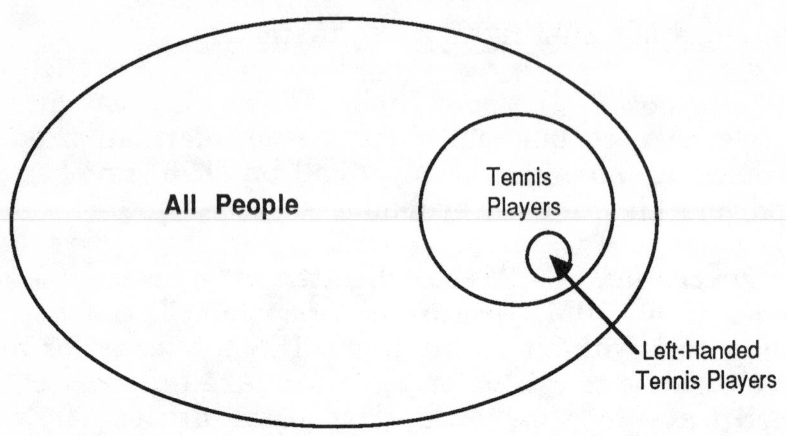

Direct mail is ideal when you are trying to target a select market, such as left-handed tennis players.

If you were to advertise your new tennis racket in your local newspaper (even in the sports section), you would still be reaching a lot of people — some of whom would be left-handed — who are not tennis players.

If, on the other hand, you took out an ad in *Tennis* magazine, you would be sure to reach tennis players, but most of them would be right-handed.

By using direct mail, however, you could hopefully obtain a list of left-handed tennis players in the United States. Even though it would cost you significantly more per person, at least you would know that your sales message was being received by the right audience.

Here is more relevant example of this targeting. Say you just listed a famous celebrity's home, with an asking price of $2.6 million.

Would you take out a full-page ad in the real estate section of the local giveaway "Penny Saver," or would you target a more affluent audience?

Personal Medium

Unlike many other marketing avenues, direct mail is very personal. You, as the marketer, can speak directly to your prospect, typically in the privacy of his or her own home.

In addition, a "you-and-me" style of copy works well since mail, by nature, is personal.

Many people play down this "personal" factor, but a good direct-mail piece needs to be personal.

Uncluttered Medium

As consumers, we are bombarded by advertising. Wake up in the morning, and your clock radio broadcasts up to 15 one-minute "spots" per hour — in between news, weather, traffic, and entertainment.

Open the morning newspaper, and you have hundreds of ads competing for your attention. Turn on a morning TV news program and there are more commercials.

On your way to work, it is back to radio. In addition to those advertisements, the highway is dotted with billboard ads as well. By the time you get to work in the morning, you are "advertised" out.

Direct mail, on the other hand, has little competition. While it is true your mailbox may be full of competing mailings, if you decide to open a particular letter, you will probably look at it basically without distraction — most likely from the comfort of your favorite chair.

Full Message

Direct mail allows you to present an entire message without the limitations of other media. Most television commercials, for example, are only 30 seconds long. Those advertisements which do not have the logistical limitations of TV or radio have cost restrictions. A full-page newspaper or magazine ad, for example, will cost up to six times what a one-sixth-page ad costs.

Direct mail *is* different. While the costs do increase as you add more and more elements — such as brochures, separate letters, reply envelopes — these incremental increases are small in proportion to the entire cost of the mailing.

This is one reason many direct-mail packages often include four-page letters, multiple brochures, other supporting material, order cards, and more.

Another reason is that these added elements usually work.

Pure Mathematics

If products or services are selected properly, the mathematics will make them work in direct mail. Say that you have just created a software program designed to help realtors with their farming.

After getting a manual written and printed and finding suitable packaging, you are all set with your product. Altogether it costs you $10 per unit for the package, manual, and diskettes.

Then you go out and talk to a number of realtors and get a feel for the selling price — how much it is worth to them — which might be $80.

Conventional Retail

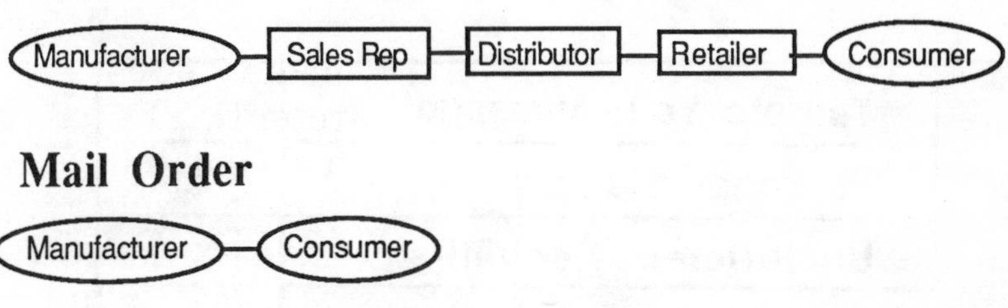

Conventional retail channels require many hands, each getting a cut of the final price. Mail order, on the other hand, leaves far more of the selling price for the manufacturer/marketer.

Now you are faced with the task of marketing it. Essentially there are two ways to go:

One is you can go through the conventional retail channels. However, retail stores will only purchase your software at 50% off the retail price.

In addition, to reach the retailers, you need to work through the distributors who supply them. They want another 15% (of the 50%-off price).

Finally, you have to hire a salesperson to get these distributors to carry it, and he or she also gets a 15% commission.

So now, instead of getting $70 profit ($80 sales price less the $10 production cost), you are only going to get about $18.90 (50% [$40] off for the retailer, 15% [$6] off for the distributor, another 15% [$5.10] off the distributor's price for the salesperson you hired, and, of course, you still have your $10 production costs).

Moreover, you need to advertise the product so people will go into the retail stores and buy it; and you still have to pay for any overhead and development costs you incurred. These costs must be deducted from the $18.90.

Targets Your Message	√
Personal Medium	√
Uncluttered Medium	√
Full & Complete Message	√
Pure Mathematics	√
Tracked Response	√

Elements of Success in Direct Marketing — The above items are the main reasons why direct mail works for real estate farming.

The second way to market your software would be by mail. In this case, you would take out a couple of ads in the leading real estate magazines or rent mailing lists of realtors who own computers.

While the costs of these ads may appear high at first, the $70 profit on each order they produce will help pay for them.

Response Can Easily Be Tracked

Finally, and perhaps most important, direct mail allows you to track the response. Each time you do a mailing or place an ad, you can code it so that you know exactly how many orders or leads each ad or mailing generated.

By doing this, it is easy to keep an account of costs

and revenues and make sure that your costs are paying their bills, and then some, on the revenue side.

Why Direct Mail Works for Real Estate

Targeted Message

As covered in Chapter 2, farming requires targeting your select market, or what real estate professionals call a farm. Using the mail (versus other media methods, such as newspapers and radio) allows you this pinpoint accuracy.

Personal Medium

What is more personal than one's home? Your message about your prospects' homes reaches them at their homes, and when they have plenty of time to evaluate it in a very personal setting.

Uncluttered Medium

There is plenty of competition out there on the real estate front. The real estate sections of your weekend newspapers are filled with competing ads. Direct mail lets you speak to your prospects one-on-one, standing head and shoulders above the crowd.

Full Message

As you know, a person's home is almost always the biggest financial investment he or she will ever make. When making a decision regarding such an important matter, a full and complete sales message is needed.

Pure Mathematics

This is the most significant factor in why direct mail works for real estate.

And it means looking at the value of a prospect, which you will see in the next chapter. But briefly, if you got just one additional listing from your direct mail farming, worth a gross commission of $3,750 (as calculated in Chapter 2), that could pay for the typical direct-mail costs for monthly mailings to a farm of 1,000 homes for an entire year!

More on this in the next chapter.

Response Can Easily Be Tracked

Finally, and especially important when you are first starting out in direct mail farming, you can quite easily track your responses, thus knowing for certain if your direct-mail farming is paying off.

By coding the reply devices and other response mechanisms (as will be covered later in this book), you can track and assign costs with returns.

This response tracking and testing is the cornerstone of traditional direct-mail marketing.

Summary

In this chapter you looked at many of the basics of direct mail. This will serve as a foundation for future chapters in which you will examine in detail the specific applications for real estate.

Initially, the term "direct marketing" was defined, and then the chapter went on to detail the tremendous growth of this medium.

From there, you looked at the common types of direct mail and compared and contrasted one-step (direct sales) versus two-step (lead generation).

In addition, you saw some of the reasons direct mail works and why it works so well for real estate:

- Targeted sales messages
- Personal and uncluttered marketing method
- The fact that it can deliver a full message
- Its pure mathematics
- And, finally, its trackability

Now it is time to begin *your* direct-mail farming.

Part II

All About Direct-Mail Farming

4. Strategies for Direct-Mail Farming Success

Before getting started with your direct-mail farming program, it is important to first sit down and consider your objectives, as well as your costs.

To begin, you must look at the value of a customer.

How Much a Customer Is Worth

If your average *net* commission on a listing is $1,875 (half the gross commission of $3,750, as calculated in Chapter 2, with the other half going to your broker), then that means if you got only one additional listing per year from your direct-mail farm efforts, you would make a "profit" from them as long as your direct-mail expenses did not exceed that $1,875.

To illustrate how many direct-mail pieces you could mail with $1,875, divide it by the estimated cost per piece mailed. In this case, use 35¢ per piece mailed to get 5,357.14 pieces, or approximately 5,350 pieces per year.

Now, a good, consistent direct-mail farming program should consist of mailings at least every six weeks and, ideally, every month.

So if you do monthly mailings, then divide this 5,350 by 12 to get approximately 445 pieces per month.

This means if you *only* get one additional listing per year from your direct-mail farming, then it would pay you to mail to as many as 445 homes.

In other words, your "break-even" monthly farm size is 445 if you only get one additional listing per year from you farm efforts.

If you get four additional listings per year from your direct-mail farming efforts, then your break-even point moves to over 1,780 homes per month, and so on.

This break-even point should be your absolute minimum; hopefully, these efforts will generate significant profits from your farm.

Broker Co-Op

The break-even analysis calculated above was based on your net commission after your broker-agent split. However, since they will be sharing in the profits of your direct-mail farm efforts, many brokers will also share the costs.

Logically, if they split commissions 50/50, then they should split costs 50/50 as well. Of course, if they are not totally sold on direct-mail farming, then perhaps they will not.

But even if the broker just paid for the bulk-mail postage, this would give the agent more potential profits from the same size mailings.

For example, your out-of-pocket expenses drop from

35¢ per piece down to 22.5¢ per piece if the broker picks up the tab on the bulk-mail postage. This means it will only cost *you* $1,203.75 to mail the same 5,350 pieces per year. Instead of just breaking even (assuming you get just one more listing per year) your profits are up $671.25 ($1,875 net commission less $1,203.75 in costs).

The broker, too, has done well. Even though he or she picked up the tab for the $671.25 bulk-mail postage, he or she also got $1,875 in net commissions, less the $671.25 for a profit of $1,203.75.

In this case the broker just assumed a portion of the costs. If the broker assumed them to the amount that he or she participated in their revenues, then the true break-even analysis for your direct-mail farming program would be based on the gross commissions to the office (i.e., agent *and* broker commissions), not just yours as the agent.

Establishing a Budget

Before you embark on a direct-mail farming program, you need to figure out a rough budget — something you as an agent can present to your broker, or you as a broker can discuss with your agent.

Mailing Costs

Actual per-piece mailing costs will vary depending on what goes into the mailing; but 30¢ to 35¢ will cover a pretty complete mail piece — including bulk-mail postage, envelopes, cover letters, insert-brochures, and reply devices (all of which will be discussed later).

For this next example again estimate mailing costs at 35¢ per piece.

You figured your farm size in Chapter 2, based on income goals and other ratios, to be 328 homes.

To find the total mailing cost per mailing, simply multiply the cost per piece by the number of pieces mailed:

$.35 per piece x 328 pieces per mailing = $114.80 per mailing

Now the only thing left to determine is the frequency with which you want to mail to your farm. As stated earlier, monthly is ideal. And if you are truly committed to farming, then at least initially you should attempt this, as in this example.

To find the total mailing cost per year, simply multiply the per-mailing cost above by the number of mailings per year:

$114.80 per mailing x 12 mailings per year = $1,377.60 per year

In summary, then, the mailing costs for your direct-mail farming efforts will be $1,377.60 for a 328-home farm, mailed 12 times a year at an average cost of 35¢ per piece mailed.

Other One-Time Costs

In addition to the mailing costs calculated above, there are several other costs associated with your direct-mail farming which you should be aware of. Some of these, however, would be incurred even without direct mailings, and others can be shared by other direct-mail farmers.

Postage Permit Fees — The US Postal Service charges annual fees for obtainingmpermits both for bulk mail and for business reply mail (prepaid mail cards and envelopes you include in your mailings so your respondents can mail back to you without having to put on a stamp). Your firm may already have these, but if not, they run approximately $100 per year.

Initial List Costs — While you can probably acquire your original mail list at no charge from your local title company or MLS, you may need to buy either "reverse" phone directories or compiled lists from outside services to get phone numbers. These are typically one-time costs, unique to the individual direct-mail farmer.

Typesetting — The preparing of letterheads, stationery, and business cards is typically expensed as an operating cost of running the brokerage office. The actual printing of them, when they are included in a mailing, is considered part of mailing costs.

However, the preparation of master newsletter formats, business reply cards and envelopes, and other common insert pieces is generally a one-time cost and is logically charged to direct mail.

Personal Computer Hardware — Personal computers are *not* required to be an effective direct-mail farmer — after all, agents have been farming by mail for a lot longer than computers have been affordable.

But let me also say that they can make your job an awful lot easier. If you already own or have access to a personal computer, or are thinking of purchasing one for other reasons as well, then it would make sense to allocate a portion of its cost to your direct-mail farming.

Personal Computer Software — There are many general mail lists and data-base management programs which are well suited to your farming needs. In addition, there are custom programs designed specifically for real estate farming which are even better. If you go out and purchase either of these types of programs, then it would make sense to charge its one-time cost to your direct-mail farming.

Manual Aids — Whether you use a personal computer or not, you will probably end up buying (or having printed) some farming supplies, such as index cards, a farm file, maps, directories, and rubber stamps. Here, use your judgement with regard to cost allocation.

Printing Equipment — Before going out and buying high-speed duplicating machines, remember that your local instant printer is probably better equipped to handle your needs.

While an office copier may be fine for making a couple of quick copies of a deposit receipt or lease payment schedule, it is not made for relatively big print runs. And quality, which reflects on your image, suffers. In addition, you will often want to include in your mailing things like a second color (other than black) and odd sizes (for reply cards, etc.).

For what you get, your local printer is usually a very good value.

Premiums (Free Gifts) — From time to time, you may want to include free gifts either with your mailing or as a follow-up to a response. The costs for these are hard to estimate since you will most likely want to try a few and will only continue using them if the results merit it. Still, it is something you should be aware of, and you should make a rough estimate at the start.

Miscellaneous — Finally, there are always miscellaneous supplies, etc., which you will end up buying for your farm needs. It is important to keep track of these for profitability analysis later.

Nonmonetary Considerations

Outside of the budget and cost considerations, getting started is the best way to evaluate your own commitment to successful farming by mail.

It will take some time, especially when you first get started, to put together and maintain your farm mailing list. There will also be some initial costs, though most of these are not tremendous.

Moreover, there will be times when your mailings fail to generate any leads whatsoever. These are the trying times that beg you to give it up in favor of more emphasis on personal or telephone contact.

Initially you must ask yourself this very simple question: Am I committed to giving my best effort to farming by mail for a period of at least one year? If, after careful consideration, the answer is yes, then forge ahead; you are ready to start planting the seeds.

Summary

This chapter looked at the overall cost and return associated with farming by mail. First and most important was the "value of a customer" (or a listing, in the case of real estate farming).

This led to a simple break-even analysis on the annual cost of making monthly mailings to a farm of 328 homes.

You also read about broker co-ops, or the sharing of direct-mail costs between the agent and the commission-sharing broker.

Then the chapter took a quick look at some of the one-time, nonrecurring costs of getting started.

And finally, you were asked the book's most important question — one you must ask yourself before beginning: Am I committed to giving my best effort to farming by mail for a period of at least one year?

And hopefully you answered yes!

5. Your Farm Mailing List

As mentioned in the last chapter, creating your mailing list may be the most tedious and time-consuming task you will perform. Fortunately, you only have to do it once.

Getting Your Original Mailing List

Social Farms

If you choose a social farm, your job of creating a mailing list will either be greatly simplified or made overly cumbersome.

Most clubs and organizations keep their own mailing lists of members, and many make these available in the form of regular directories of members. If they do not publish a directory, you can usually gain access to the list as long as you are a member in good standing.

Then you just convert this membership listing into a usable format for your farming needs, generally eliminating some names such as competing realtors.

If your club or organization does not maintain such a listing, you might recommend they do. In fact, you might even volunteer to create it for them.

On the other hand, if there is no way to quickly get these names, then you are in for a lot of hard work. Typically, you would have to manually go through the members' names in the local telephone book and prepare the entire listing yourself.

If you can, avoid this at all cost.

Territorial Farms

If you are planning to set up a territorial farm, your local title company or MLS should be able to help you out by providing a complete address list of your prospective farm territory — in some cases, on pre-printed labels. Most title companies will provide this service to real estate agents and brokers for no charge or for a very nominal fee.

However, this data will not normally contain phone numbers, which you will need for your telephone follow-up. To get these phone numbers, you can either go through your local directory manually or obtain a reverse phone directory, which lists phone numbers in address order rather than by the occupant's last name.

In addition to data provided by title companies, you may be able to get a list (often with phone numbers included) of residents in a joint homeowners association, such as for a condominium project.

If title company or MLS data is not available to you, you may set up a list using the reverse directory or through an outside mail list service. Such firms can be found in your Yellow Pages under the heading

"Mailing Lists." The biggest problem with using these services is that they typically serve much larger mailers and usually have minimums of 3,000 to 5,000 names — which means if you only need 500 names, you are going to have to pay a premium to get them.

Additionally, the industry trade practice is to "rent" names on a one-time-only basis rather than purchase them outright. However, most compilers of general lists, such as homeowners by specific zip codes, will make arrangements to sell you the list, but it tends to be costly.

A final consideration about dealing with an outside list compiler, which also applies to reverse phone directories, is that there is a time lag between when the information was collected and when it is published.

Luckily, as you will discover later in this chapter, you can easily update the list with your initial mailing to your new farm.

Manual Lists

If you do not have a computer, then you must keep your list by hand. In order to do this, you will need an index card file and peel-off mailing label sheets for which you type a master on blank paper and then have it reproduced by your quick printer onto labels — unless, of course, you can obtain label or label-format names directly from your source (title company or MLS).

One way to do a manual list is to type the labels first (in zip code order on the master) and then produce one extra copy to stick on the index cards. This saves some considerable writing and duplication of effort.

You type the master labels in zip code order because the post office requires this for bulk mail.

Another important thing to keep in mind is the accuracy of name spelling and other things associated with the labels. If you misspell a prospect's name on the original label, then the first thing that person will see from you will be incorrect. How do you think this reflects on your real estate marketing skills?

Since most people have difficulty in proofing their own work, try to get someone else to help you.

Your master index card file should be kept in alphabetical order so you can easily access cards when your farm prospects call in.

As you work your farm, you will want to add prospect and property information to the data card, so leave room for this additional information, which might go on the back side of your farm card.

Manual Farm Form

Joe Prospect
123 Way Street
Anytown, USA 12345

Phone Number ________________

Husband's Job ____________ Wife's Job __________

Interests __________________________________

Kids ______________________________________

Type of House ______________________________

First Contact Date ___________ (see next contact on back)

Category ________ Comments _________________

An example of a manual farm form with the mailing label pasted in the upper right-hand corner.

Computerized Lists

As covered earlier, personal computers are not necessary for mail list creation and maintenance, but they are helpful.

The software you choose should be simple and easy to use so you need not spend hours learning how to run it.

Specific programs for real estate farming (of which there are several commercially available) can speed up the learning curve. However, since real estate farm mailing lists are not complicated for a computer, readily available data-base or mail-list management programs ought to do the job for you.

When you first work with a mail list program, you will probably come across two important, and possibly confusing, terms: "records" and "fields."

To simplify, a record is all the data associated with a single prospect's information. In the simplest case this would include: name, address, city, state, *and* zip code.

A field is one of these elements, such as the name, address, city, state, *or* zip code.

In short, fields make up records, and records are composed of fields.

Computer manuals also talk about "sortable" and "nonsortable" fields.

At the very least, you want to be able to sort by last name (for your master file) and by zip code (for your postage). Other fields that make sense to allow sorting include: street name, city (if you have more than one in your farm), last and next contact dates (for personal or phone contact), and perhaps some miscellaneous fields such as property type (i.e., rooms, square footage, and schools).

When creating fields for your records (if you are modifying a non-real estate mail list or data-base program), always include an extra short (sortable) field or two for classifying your prospects. You may not need them at first, but many programs will not let you add them later when you do need them.

As for the labels, your local computer supply store sells special labels which fit into the printer's tractor feed and which are standard widths and lengths. These typically come in one-, two-, three-, or four-across sizes. Look through your software manual to find which it recommends — four-across labels are usually the cheapest per label.

As for creating a master (index card) file, you may not have to. Many of these programs let you print master rosters or specialized forms to manually maintain and update your prospects. If not, you can at least sort the farm file by last name before printing out the labels, thus saving some manual sorting.

One final note about computer programs is one probably heard hundreds of times, but it is worth repeating.

Make a backup of your data and store it in a safe place!

Thousands upon thousands of people have lost a lot of hard work and information due *not* to computer failure — but their own failure to properly back up their data.

In short, the more time you spend creating something (such as a farm mail list) on your computer, the more vital it is that your properly back it up.

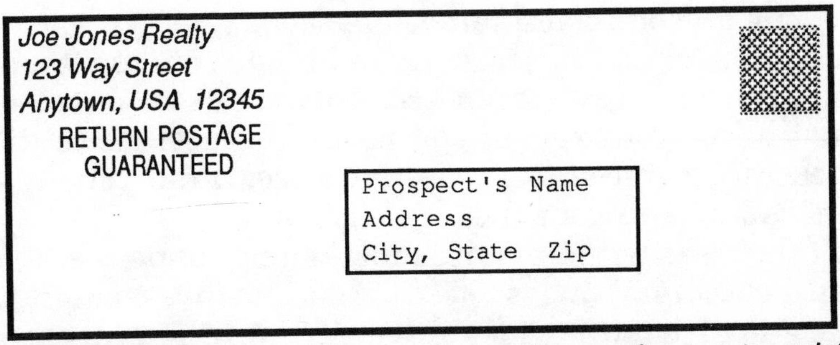

Joe Jones Realty
123 Way Street
Anytown, USA 12345
RETURN POSTAGE
GUARANTEED

Prospect's Name
Address
City, State Zip

Cleaning Your List — With your first mailing, make sure to update your list by using the endorsement "Return Postage Guaranteed" if you don't need the former occupant's new address if he or she has moved.

Cleaning Your List with Your First Mailing

Once you create your farm mailing list and have it either on computer or on manual labels, you are only part of the way there. The data which you used to create the master list may or may not have been accurate or timely, especially if it came from a non-real estate source such as a reverse directory or mail list company. So with your first mailing, you may need to update or "clean" your mailing list.

The US Postal Service offers two services to aid in this: Return Postage Guaranteed and Address Correction.

Return Postage Guaranteed

When you start a farm and you do not already know the prospects, as might be the case with a territorial farm, you want to know which names on your list are no longer good so you can delete them.

To do this, you simply add the endorsement "Return Postage Guaranteed" to your outer envelope (just below your return address). The post office will then return these to you — for a fee, mind you — so you can update your files.

(You see, without an endorsement, undeliverable third-class mail is destroyed. And undeliverable first-class mail is either forwarded, if the recipient has a forwarding address on file, or returned to you, if he or she does not).

Address Correction Requested

Address Correction Requested works along the same lines but would be used if you wanted to obtain the new address (i.e., where the homeowner moved to), as might be the case with a social farm.

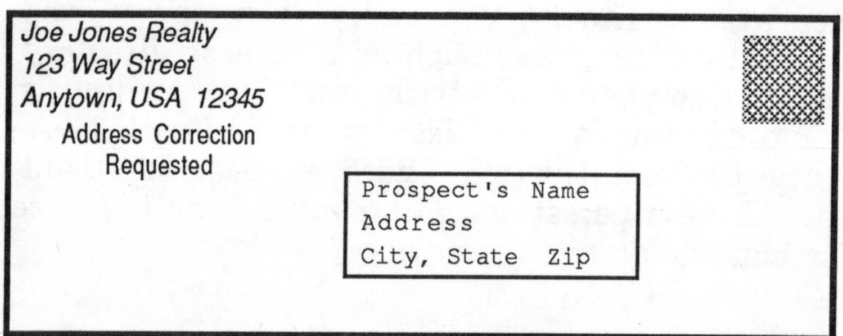

Cleaning Your List — With your first mailing, make sure to update your list by using Address Correction Requested if you need the new address. The difference between this and Return Postage Guaranteed is that you get the recipient's new address — and there is an additional fee for this service.

Here you print (or stamp) the words "Address Correction Requested" just below your name and return address, and for an additional fee you will get the new address or the reason for nondeliverability with your returned mail piece.

The primary difference between the two services is that with Return Postage Guaranteed you only get the piece back, while with Address Correction Requested you get the new address or reason for nondeliverability. In addition, the fee for this latter service on bulk mail is higher.

Specific postal requirements for first-class, bulk, and business reply mail will be covered later in this book.

Maintaining Your Farm Mailing List

Once you have created and updated your farm mailing list, you are charged with a most important task — maintaining it!

Your farm list, if it is well maintained, will be one of your most important business assets, and you should treat it that way.

Maintaining the list, whether on your manual cards or on a personal computer, takes a lot of work. You should add bits of information each time you talk with or read about a person in your farm. Things like promotions, birth and wedding announcements, and property changes are important facts about your farm which you will want to include.

When you are first starting out, make certain that in talking with each member of your farm you get basic data such as how long they have lived in the neighborhood, number and ages of children, details on their properties, and their likes and dislikes.

This will serve as a foundation for maintaining this most precious asset — your farm list.

In addition, you should be on top of your farm enough not to require the US Postal Service updates on change of address, etc.; but it never hurts to double-check by requesting them in your mailings.

Remember, direct mail is just one facet of a comprehensive farming effort. Let it work for you and your real estate profitability.

Summary

This chapter covered the process of creating a farm mailing list. It can be a very tedious task, yet may be greatly simplified with help from your title company or MLS.

You can maintain a farm list one of two ways — manually, using index cards and a farm file, or on computer. As personal computers have become more affordable (and more powerful), their use in the real estate business has increased dramatically .

But they are not a requirement for farming by mail.

Another thing to remember when first putting your mail list together is that the information you use to create the list may or may not be current or correct. This is especially true if you are using outside, non-real estate sources for a territorial farm.

What you should do, then, is make an initial mailing to clean or update your master farm file. You should not be surprised if 10% to 15% of your list contains bad data, especially if you used a third-party source (such as a reverse phone directory). People, as you well know, move frequently.

Once you have done this initial mailing, make the corrections to your list and get the current names (or current addresses) correctly inserted.

Finally, once you have a clean list of names, you need to maintain it vigorously and add pertinent bits of information as you talk with your prospects either by phone or in person. If you do this on an ongoing basis, it will take just a few minutes of your time each month and pay you back handsomely.

If you work on your farm, your farm will work for you.

6. What to Mail to Your Farm

The greatest amount of direct mail currently done by real estate professionals has to be in the form of regular newsletters. Most mail them as a self-mailer (mailed as one piece with no envelope), but some enclose them in an envelope and even add some elements of a sales letter.

Newsletters Versus Sales Letters

It is strange how the newsletter has evolved to its current popularity. I see no logical reason for it, other than the fact that so many people are already mailing them.

Unlike the classic sales letter, the newsletter offers no real way to generate a lead.

For the most part, newsletters are public relations oriented rather than sales oriented.

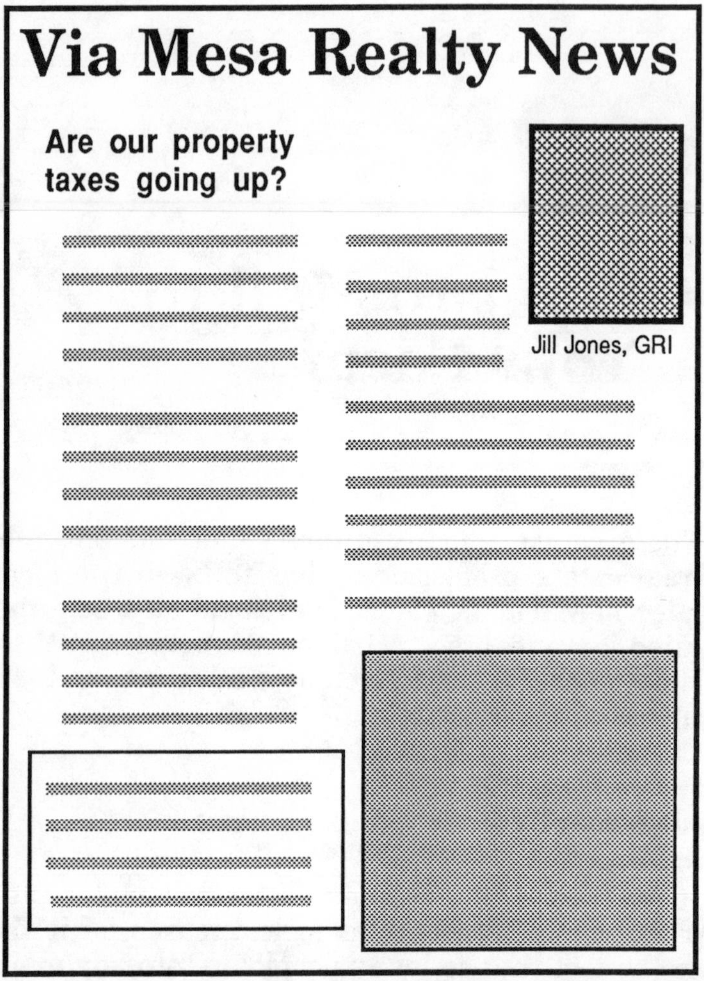

Via Mesa Realty News

Are our property taxes going up?

Jill Jones, GRI

The most popular type of mailing done by real estate professionals — newsletters — normally offers no method of generating leads. However, they do serve a public relations purpose.

Sure, everyone needs public relations; but as a salesperson, you have a far greater need for good, prequalified leads.

Certainly you can create a response-directed newsletter, but why bother, since the classic direct-mail sales letter is far better suited for garnering leads from your farm.

On the other hand, newsletters still serve a purpose, and you will want to get the most from them as well. There are two ways to publish a newsletter: (1) do it yourself or (2) buy a preproduced one.

Like many things in life, you are far better off producing a newsletter yourself.

Producing Your Own Newsletter

However, making your own newsletter is a lot of work. Not only do you have to find ideas for it, but you must write it, edit it, have it typed or typeset, and produce it.

And repeat that process several times a year!

Furthermore, if it comes out anything less than professional, you may hurt your image rather than improve it.

Cost factors, too, come into play with producing your own newsletters. If you choose to have it professionally typeset, you will probably spend between $100 and $150 just for the artwork; that cost would amount to about 50¢ per piece for a 300-home farm.

Typed newsletters will save you in preparation costs, but they look less professional — which is not always bad.

A well-written typed newsletter with interesting local news and tidbits — *including your recent listings, sales, and open houses* — will be far better received than a professionally prepared newsletter with no local interest.

Your farm residents have access to all the national news and interesting facts they want with such publications as *Time, Money,* and *People.*

The information they cannot easily get is local news. And to them, your specialty is relating how local news will affect them as homeowners — remember, you are their real estate expert.

And if you can produce a newsletter that consistently provides "expert" local real estate news, then you have a winning newsletter, worth its weight in platinum.

Other local information you can include in your newsletter is:

- Personal interest stories about people in your neighborhood
- Neighborhood events and functions
- Free classified ads for sales and services
- Your own sales and listings

Then you can fill the balance of your newsletter with "stock" items, such as gardening tips, recipes, and anecdotes. Even stock items can be given a local flavor — i.e., Joyce Williams' apple pie recipe or gardening pointers from Sam's Nursery.

Preproduced Newsletters

This critical local news, unfortunately, is where the stock commercial newsletters fall short.

Currently several firms provide such newsletters (for a fee), and they fall into two categories: (1) firms that provide the finished printed newsletter (you send them a photo and your logo or letterhead) and (2) firms that create master newsletter art which you then take to your local printer who adds your logo and photo.

This latter format allows for some flexibility, and if nothing else, the general information they supply can fill in the gaps between local news.

The cost for either type of service is not bad.

The finished newsletter firms make their money on being able to make large print runs, thus lowering the per-unit cost. And the master artwork firms make their money, of course, on the actual sale.

This is not meant to condemn newsletter services. For many professionals, this is the only form of direct mail farming they do — and it is far better than doing nothing.

Public relations does serve a purpose in farming.

(At the end of this chapter, you will find a list of several newsletter firms that provide preproduced newsletters.)

The Classic Direct-Mail Sales Letter Package

In contrast to the newsletter, you have the sales letter.

If you look at your own mailbox — and as a direct-mail farmer you should — you will see that most sales-oriented mailings consist of contents mailed in an envelope. The type, color, and size of the envelopes vary greatly, but it is this envelope which defines its classic format.

The elements of a classic package, besides the outer

envelope, often include: a letter, order card, response envelope, brochure, and sometimes a free gift.

Outer Envelope

The outer envelope is obviously what the prospect will see first. It is from this, and this alone, that he or she will decide whether to open the letter or throw it in the trash. And that decision — which will make or break a mailing — takes but a second or two.

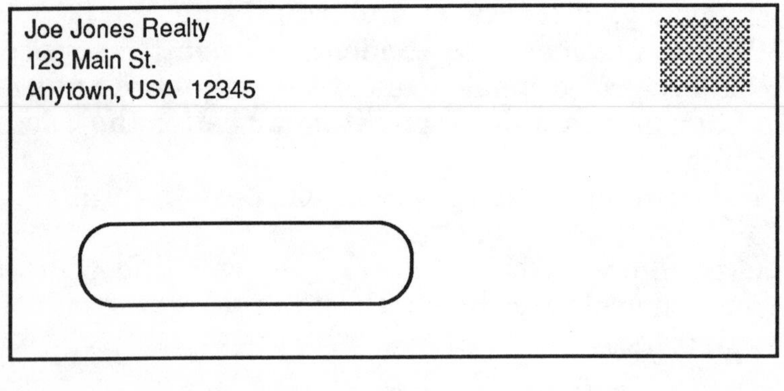

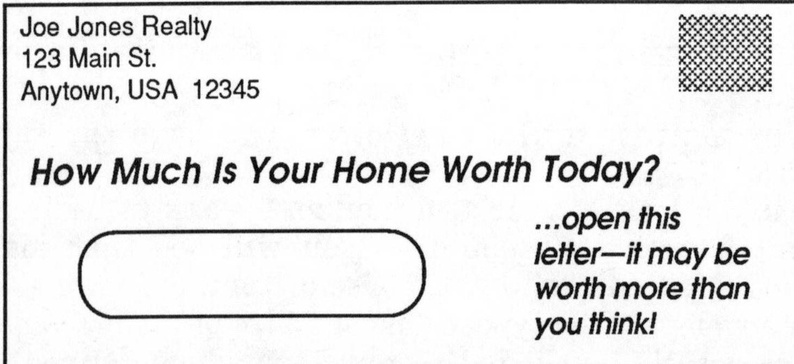

Teaser copy on the outer envelope or not? The right appeal will help get the envelope opened, while the wrong one will hurt.

One of the biggest debates in direct mail has not to do with size, shape, or coloration of envelopes, but whether to include an ad or "teaser" copy on them or to send them blank (with only a return address).

The blank envelope is the safest route, since it is least obviously "junk mail."

On the other hand, if you study the direct mail you receive, you will notice most of it has copy on the outer envelope. Be forewarned, however, that at direct-mail ad agencies — the firms which produce most of the mailings you get — it is only the most skilled copywriters and creative directors who are assigned to write outer envelope copy.

Teaser envelope copy is no job for a novice.

Letter

Many direct-mail experts consider the letter the most important element inside a successful direct-mail package. Letters can vary in length from a brief note to an 8- to 10-page detailed letter. Most commonly they are 1 to 4 pages long.

Usually the letter is typewritten (or has the appearance of being typewritten) and is written in very personal "you-and-me" style.

Most of them start out with a salutation, such as "Dear Neighbor" or "Dear Real Estate Professional," and immediately move to the single most important benefit of what the offer will do for the reader.

From there, the letter expands to a close and a call for some kind of action — either a sale or follow-up. A well-written direct-mail letter should be able to stand on its own merits, with the other elements of the direct-mail package serving as supporting material.

☐ Yes! I'd like to find out how much my home is worth today. Please set me up for a Home Market Review!
The best time to reach me is ________

Preprinted label with respondent's name, etc.

Thank you!

A good reply device should be easy to fill out and clearly state the offer presented.

Order or Response Card

The second most important piece inside a mail package is the order or response card. Generally they are either preaddressed, postage-paid cards or similar cards which you enclose in a preaddressed, postage-paid envelope.

These should be simple to fill out and require very little effort on the part of the respondent. And most important, they should restate the biggest benefit of the offer presented.

Brochure

A brochure or additional insert can be anything you want, such as an ad or piece of research material prepared by your affiliation headquarters marketing department, the National Association of Realtors, your local board, or even yourself.

It should be meaningful and help explain any potentially unclear points in your mail presentation. Also, it should serve to strengthen your position in the recipient's mind.

One powerful insert idea commonly used in other direct-mail applications is a testimonial sheet. To put one together, contact several past clients and see if they are willing to have you quote them — most people will be. Then prepare a one-page sheet with your picture on top and their (briefly) quoted comments (including name and city) below.

Hearing good things about you from someone else is stronger than hearing them from you.

Premiums

The use of premiums, or free gifts, in direct mail — as well as in personal farming — is a testy subject to say the least. Everyone wonders whether they should try them.

The cost of a premium can be 5 to 10 times the cost of your basic mailing, so you want to make sure you select the right premium.

You can use either of two different types: front-end or back-end premiums.

Front-End Premiums

A front-end premium is one that you mail with the initial direct-mail package. Examples include: pens, small writing pads, pot holders, and the like. When selecting a front-end premium, be sure it is mailable and will not greatly increase the cost of your outbound postage.

Perhaps the biggest single benefit of front-end premiums is that they make the direct-mail package unique. If you got three similar-looking bulk-mail envelopes in your mailbox and one had something like a pen in it, which would you open?

Back-End Premiums

Back-end premiums require the respondent to take some course of action in order to obtain the premium — most often, to return a card.

Back-end premiums are good ways to open the doors to hard-to-reach homes in your farm, and you might use them extensively for this purpose. Generally they carry a larger perceived value, and since only a minority will respond, you can afford to spend a little extra on them.

A book on the new tax law, a homeowner's record-keeping kit, or a "Free Market Review" are classic examples of back-end premiums used by real estate professionals.

Be advised that while these back-end premiums may lift the response quantity, quality may suffer. Some people will do just about anything to get something for free. Luckily, with a list as small as a real estate farmer's, you may isolate these individuals if necessary.

If you go to the trouble of offering a premium, make sure the people to whom you mail know it. With a lot of front-end premiums, the package itself will let the recipients know something unique is inside.

With back-end premiums you may have to announce it on the envelope.

The final word on premiums is that they are usually worth trying. If you plan to mail to your farm 12 times a year, why not try one of each type (front-end and back-end) early on to see how they do?

Self-Mailer

The other direct-mail format is the self-mailer. It does not get mailed in an outer envelope, but rather as a single piece.

Normally it is one printed piece folded and addressed directly on a back panel. It lacks the involvement of a classic direct-mail package and typically costs less — although some complex formats can be quite costly.

Self-mailers are quick and easy to work with, since there is only one element to create and print (and no inserting to worry about); but this savings in time and money will often cost you more in the long run as response rates for self-mailers rarely match those of classic packages.

But like everything, they have their place.

Many people use this format to mail their newsletters, which is its best application for real estate farming.

Summary

In this chapter you looked at the difference between the newsletter, which is public relations oriented, and the sales letter, which is sales oriented.

Both have their place, but in farming by mail you are more concerned with generating high-quality leads for follow-up action.

The sales letter, which you will look at in detail later, is far better suited for getting you these leads.

If you decide to distribute a newsletter, then you can either do it yourself, or use one of the commercial real estate newsletter publishers.

Despite the work involved, you are far better off putting out your own newsletter, rather than paying for newsletters which will have no local interest to your farm.

The chapter also covered one of the basics of direct mail: format.

The two formats that apply to real estate farming are the classic direct-mail package (sent in an envelope) and the self-mailer (sent as one piece).

Both, of course, have their place in direct mail, but the classic package has shown, over the years, that it generally pulls better response. However, the trade-off is its higher cost and the work required to print several pieces and have them inserted and sealed in an envelope.

Firms That Publish Newsletters for Real Estate:

The Austin Group
PO Box 656
Shawnee Mission, Kansas 66201
1-913-492-0377

Kall Publications
2701 Alcott, Suite 282
Denver, Colorado 80211
1-303-455-7928

MoneyTalk Publishing, Inc.
PO Box 3205
Walnut Creek, California 94598
1-415-825-4644

Newsletter Services, Inc.
PO Box 3428
Littleton, Colorado 80161
1-303-694-1248

The Personal Marketing Co.
8520 Sweetwater, Suite F57
Houston, Texas 77037
1-713-591-6015

Professional Newsletters
33082 Sea Bright Drive
Dana Point, California 92629
1-714-496-8425

Part III

Words That Make Money

7. Introduction to Copywriting

"Copy" is the words used to communicate your sales message to your audience, in this case your farm. And it is vital to your mailing's success or failure.

John Caples, vice-president of the ad agency Batten, Barton, Durstine & Osborn, describes in his book *Tested Advertising Methods* (Reward Books, 1974), two ads which were identical in every way except for the copy. One of the ads generated 19.5 times as many sales as the other.

What this says in a nutshell is that copy is critically important.

Appeal to Human Wants and Needs

Most important in your writing, you must motivate people by appealing to their human wants and needs.

Much research has been conducted on the topic of human motivation, and rightly so. It is vital to any kind of sales effort.

Dr. Abraham Maslow developed one of the most noteworthy and studied theories, and one that is very applicable to direct-mail sales letters.

In a nutshell, Maslow's Hierarchy of Needs says that people are motivated by their own needs. And he classified those needs into five levels of importance in ascending order:

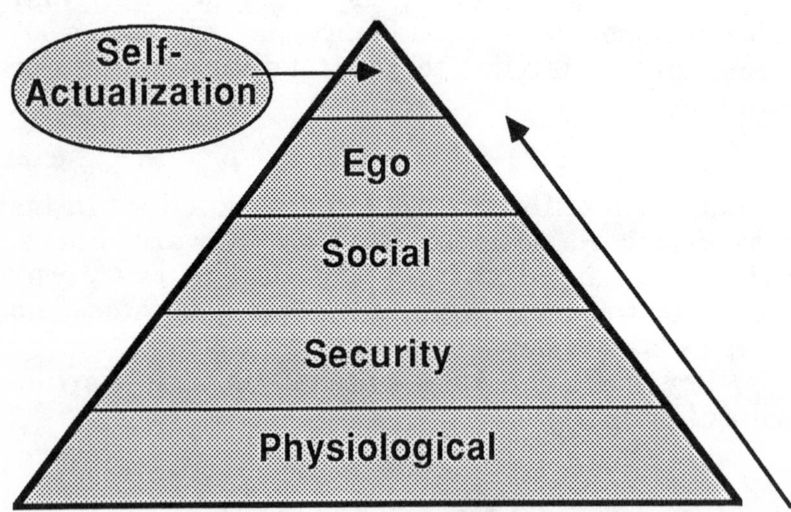

Maslow's Hierarchy of Needs — This long-studied theory of human motivation says that people are motivated by their needs. The five levels (as presented above) are presented in ascending order of importance. And once one level is met, such as Physiological needs, a person then moves up to the next higher level, Security.

1. *Physiological Needs — food, shelter, clothing*
2. *Security Needs — protection*
3. *Social Needs — belonging and association*
4. *Ego Needs — accomplishment, status*
5. *Self-Actualization — reaching one's own potential*

Dr. William Cohen, author of *Building a Mail Order Business,* notes that once one level of needs is satisfied, it no longer motivates a person's behavior; and second, if a need is for some reason not met, it becomes of extreme importance to that person.

Four Motivators of the 1980s

In his book, *Direct mail copy that sells!,* Herschell Gordon Lewis presents what he calls the "four great motivators for the mid-1980s":

- *Fear*
- *Guilt*
- *Greed*
- *Exclusivity*

It is these motivators, he argues, that should guide all of your sales writing.

Fear

Fear is the most potent motivator, since it underscores all of what we do in the 1980s. Fear of failure, fear of not being accepted, and fear of missing an opportunity are the main three.

Fear	Greed
Guilt	Exclusivity

Direct-mail expert Herschell Gordon Lewis says there are four great motivators — Fear, Greed, Guilt, and Exclusivity — which should guide your writing of a sales letter.

Here is an example of using fear as a motivator:

"You may be missing the best opportunity in the past decade to sell your home for a profit and move into a new one."

Greed

The preceding sentence could apply to greed as well. Greed is easy to seek out:

"If you sign up now, we'll waive the normal $25 service charge."

Guilt

Again it is easy to apply the guilt appeal. For

example:

"If you miss this opportunity, it may not come back for another 10 years."

Exclusivity

Exclusivity is also quite easy to appeal to. For example:

"Dear Preferred Client"

Or,

"Frankly, I wouldn't tell just anybody this, but you're special to me."

All four of these motivators can be in the same sales appeal, but sometimes this clouds the issue — you say a lot without saying anything.

So as you read through the copy of your sales letters and other writings to your farm, make sure the underlying motivation is based on human needs.

Making the Right Offer

The offer, or proposition, is the cornerstone of direct mail copy. Bob Stone, called by some the "father of modern direct-mail marketing," presented in his book, *Successful Direct Marketing Methods* (Crain Books, 1979), three ways to state the same thing that got entirely different responses.

The right offer makes a difference. All three offers above say the same thing, but #2 did 40% better than the other two.

The three offers he presented were:

1. Half Price!
2. Buy One—Get One *Free!*
3. 50% Off!

Each is in essence the same, but they are perceived differently by our prospects, as evidenced by the fact that statement number 2 pulled 40% better than statement numbers 1 or 3.

Unique and Personal

A good offer must be unique and personal. This is fairly easy to do in real estate because, outside of other farmers, no one is mailing them competing offers. Furthermore, direct mail, which reaches your prospect at his or her home, is a very personal medium by itself.

Perceived Value

In addition, the offer must have real *value* in the eyes of your prospective homeowners. A free pen with your name on it has very limited value, but a complete report on the effects of a new property tax change might be perceived as having considerable value to many homeowners.

Kinds of Real Estate Offers

There are several popular offers used by real estate professionals, some of which you probably do right now but perhaps not by mail.

Free Home Evaluation is one of the strongest, since it has both perceived value by a homeowner and also allows you to personally meet with your prospects and gather pertinent information about them and their homes.

In addition, it tends to appeal to the right kind of prospect (someone concerned about the value of his or her home) without the harshness of a direct listing solicitation.

Furthermore, it is not that uncommon for a Free Home Evaluation to lead to a quick listing.

Home-Seller's Kits are also popular, generally as a back-end premium. In 1986, the National Association of Realtors bound one into an issue of *Real Estate Today* magazine. It is a pretty good offer, since again you are only going to get a response from those people who have an interest in possibly selling their homes.

Open House Invitations play on neighbors' almost innate curiosity about what is going on in their own neighborhoods. There is not a lot to these offers except to invite neighbors (and their friends) to see a home for which you already have the listing.

The side advantage to this one is that it shows your farm prospects that you are doing business nearby — this, of course, can backfire with a failed listing, but let us hope that does not happen.

Free Gifts, as discussed earlier, have a double-edged sword to them. While they may increase the quantity of response to a particular mailing, they may dilute the quality. However, as a door-opener, back-end gifts (those not sent with mailing but delivered later) often cannot be beat, especially when you are first planting seeds in your farm.

FSBO (For Sale by Owner) Conversions are also popular. Some realtors go as far as to include an entire kit to help the homeowner market his property.

With their specialized nature, these would not be used in a mass mailing to your farm; but it is good to have one ready when an FSBO sign pops up in your farm.

Direct Listing Solicitations are tricky and will greatly limit your response — but the response you get will be of high quality!

No matter what you do, no one will sign up for listing by mail, so it is still a basic two-step process — sales lead, then sale (or in this case, listing). Your carefully worded letter can ease over the harshness and open the door for a listing consultation.

Other popular offers include home sales, property

management services, income property offers, and more. The limitations to good direct mail offers for real estate are truly bounded only by your mind.

Write to Individuals, Not the Masses

The most important thing to remember when you sit down to create your direct-mail letter is that you are writing to 300 individuals, not a mass of 300.

To illustrate, here are two sample introductions. The first is written for the masses and the second to an individual.

Example 1 — Written for the Masses

Dear Neighbor:

Dozens of homes in the neighborhood have been sold in recent months for well above what their owners thought they could possibly get.

What's more, here at XYZ Realty we've sold plenty of the them. . .

Example 2 — Written to an Individual

Dear Neighbor,

Your home may well be worth more than you think. Even if you're not thinking about selling, now's a good time to at least check the current value of your home.

As your local ABC Realty advisor, I'll personally come to your home, evaluate it with you, and give you a written market comparison based on local property values.

And, of course, there's no obligation of any kind to sell or list your home . . .

Even though both these letters are mass-produced and mailed to a large audience, the second letter overcomes this problem with heavy use of the "you-and-me" style of copy.

These personal words help you communicate in an emotional and persuasive manner — they serve to strengthen the impact of your letter!

No matter how large a mailing you do, you are writing to one individual at a time.

You will also want to notice the use of the word "I" in the second letter, instead of the more generic "we" used in the first letter. Again this gets back to the point about individuals writing to other individuals.

This is *your* farm not your firm's farm. These are your customers. And while you represent ABC Realty, your efforts alone will dictate whether or not that client chooses to sell his or her home through you.

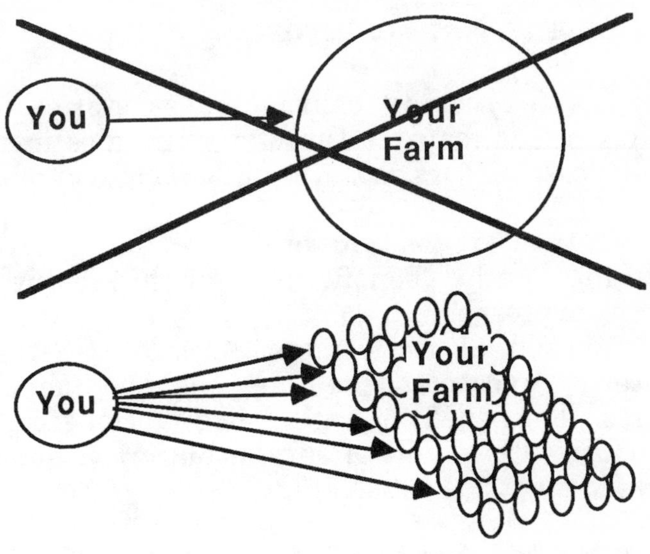

When you write to your farm, think of them as individuals, not one big mass.

Write As You Speak

Another rule of thumb in writing direct mail is to write exactly how you would speak to one person. For some strange reason, the minute people get behind a typewriter or word processor, they get tied up with format and sentence structure.

Not only does this make the task of writing far more difficult, it also impedes communication to your farm. If it helps, talk into a tape recorder before you write.

Use Benefits, Not Features

You have probably heard endless stories about benefits versus features through your sales training. Nonetheless, it bears repeating in the context of direct mail.

A "feature" is a tangible, describable part of something. And a "benefit" is what that feature will do for your prospect.

An Individual Retirement Account (IRA) is a long-term investment vehicle; that is one of its features. The benefit of an IRA is financial security.

A house with a built-in burglar alarm system offers safety from outside intruders.

Always remember, before you write to your farm, to jump into their shoes and try to read what you write from their point of view.

And do not ever overlook the obvious. Sure, they may know that burglar alarms provide safety from outside intruders; but tell them anyway.

The Long and Short of Copy

One of the most often heard sayings in conventional advertising is, "People won't read long copy."

Not true!

A mailing done awhile back for Calculated Industries again proved this point.

About a year ago the firm introduced a calculator which adds, subtracts, multiplies, and divides right in feet, inches, and fractions of an inch. It is the only one of its kind on the market, and builders have been crying for one for years.

After an initial successful mailing (with a traditional four-page, long-copy letter, brochure, testimonial sheet, small letter from the president of the company, and reply card), the firm decided to conduct a test using a boiled-down two-page letter to replace the longer one.

The thinking at the time was that since many builders were not highly educated (compared to other groups, such as lawyers and teachers) and since they also worked outside (rather than in an office), they would prefer the briefer message.

Well, that thinking was wrong.

The package which included the four-page letter pulled in over 35% more orders than the shorter counterpart. Moreover, on the average, the readers of the long letter purchased over 20% more units with their orders.

People will read long copy as long as it is interesting. A meaningless one-page letter will be trashed long before a well-written four-page letter. It is what you say and how you say it, not how many pages it takes you to say it.

Long copy lets you tell a complete story. The mail piece you send to your prospect is your only entry into his or her home at that time. If there is some unresolved question on the prospect's mind, he or she cannot ask you to clear it up. And if it goes unresolved, you have probably lost the sale.

That is why with direct mail you need to tell the full story each time.

Do not assume that your prospects will remember something you told them in the last mailing, or perhaps something from your full-page ad in last

Saturday's real estate section of the newspaper.

Tell them again.

But always tell them in a meaningful way — meaningful to them!

Don't Write Above Their Heads

The National Enquirer has one of the largest circulations of any periodical in print. If you pick one up, you will notice the words and sentences are short and simple. In fact, it is written at about a fifth-grade level.

People, *TV Guide,* and *Women's Day* are all examples of magazines that keep their grammatical structures simple — and they are very successful because of it.

Very few people want to get home from a long day at the office, open their mail, and read an essay by William F. Buckley.

According Evelyn Wood's Reading Dynamics, most people read at about a seventh-grade level. While this may be a problem for the education system, it is not your job to change it.

Your job as direct-mail writers — more specifically, as direct mail farmers — is to communicate your message.

And if writing at a seventh-grade level does that — then so be it!

After you have written your mail piece — whether it is the letter, an insert, reply piece, or anything — set it down for awhile and then pick it up and see if you can shorten or simplify the words, sentences, and paragraphs.

And if you are looking for some tips on simple

grammatical structure, go to your supermarket and pick up a copy of the *The National Enquirer.*

Avoid Using Real Estate Jargon

As a real estate professional you get used to hearing terms like "first deed of trust," "wraparound mortgages" and "exclusive right to sell" all the time.

Your farm prospects, however, do not. In fact, many of them will not even know what you are saying when you use this real estate jargon.

A recent mailing from a Pomona-area Century 21 agent highlighted this point. She offered a free silk flower arrangement "as her way of saying thanks to the first 25 homeowners who take out an "Exclusive Right to Sell" listing with her for a minimum of six months."

Her letter failed, partly because it was filled with terms such as "lockboxes," "reasonable assessment of value" and "exclusive arrangements with another licensee."

Real estate jargon has no place in your direct farm mailings.

It is always safest to keep your words simple and common to your reader.

Can You Learn to Write Direct Mail?

If you can read this book, and if you can learn to sell real estate, then you can certainly learn to write direct-mail farm letters.

Most people do not like to write nor do they believe they are good at writing. They recall horror stories from high school composition classes. But actually, sometimes this will help rather than hurt.

Good direct-mail copy, you see, does not fit well with so-called "good" grammatical prose. The same short sentences and simple structure covered earlier are the exact same things that English teachers despise.

People who have degrees in English are often poor writers of direct mail because they find themselves locked into the styles used in conventional writing.

Those who went through the business courses are more often unrestricted in their writing and, therefore, often more clear in simple communications such as direct mail.

Helpful Sources

Your library or local bookstore has many books on the topic of direct mail, as well as direct-mail ad writing.

However, there is a better source that is not only closer to home, but free — your mailbox.

Each day you receive several direct-mail offers. Instead of tossing them out, look them over carefully. Keep the ones that are unique or that peaked your interest, and study them for future reference.

Do not be afraid to borrow a phrase or two when needed. Toyota does not reinvent the wheel each time it pushes a new Camry off the assembly line.

If you want to find a sure-fire way to start getting more direct mail in your mailbox, simply respond to a few offers. Once you are found to be "direct-mail responsive," you will have all the mail you can ever handle.

Summary

This is the first chapter dealing with the most important topic of direct-mail copywriting.

The chapter began with a discussion of motivating your readers based on their human needs. Both the traditional, well-studied Maslow's Hierarchy of Needs and a more modern approach were presented.

Next came the offer, or proposition; and its importance was underscored by the example of a three-way offer — "Half Price," "Buy One, Get One Free," and "50% Off" — which proved that different ways to say the exact same thing can have entirely different results.

Good offers should be both unique and valuable in the eyes of your readers.

Several different kinds of real estate offers were then presented, many of which you may already use, but perhaps not in a direct-mail context.

Those offers include:

- *Free Home Evaluations*
- *Home-Seller's Kits*
- *Open House Invitations*
- *Free Gifts*
- *FSBO Conversions*
- *Direct Listing Solicitations*

The chapter also talked about "benefits" versus "features" in your direct-mail copy — what it will do for your prospects versus what it is.

Language, too, is important. Make sure all your words are simple and all your meanings are clear and precise; and avoid real estate jargon when you write to your farm.

And finally, you can learn and improve your direct-mail writing skills. Many fine books are available on the topic; and each day your mailbox is filled with samples you can study.

On the next page you will find a list of recommended reading on the topic of direct-mail copywriting.

Recommended Reading — Direct-Mail Copy:

Direct Mail Copy That Sells!
Herschell Gordon Lewis
Prentice Hall, Inc.
Englewood Cliffs, New Jersey

Tested Advertising Methods
John Caples
Reward Books/Prentice Hall, Inc.
Englewood Cliffs, New Jersey

Successful Direct Marketing Methods
Bob Stone
Crain Books/Crain Communications, Inc.
Chicago, Illinois

Building a Mail Order Business
William A. Cohen
John Wiley & Sons
New York, New York

The Greatest Direct Mail Sales Letters of All Time
Richard S. Hodgson
Dartnell Press/The Dartnell Corporation
Chicago, Illinois

Part IV

The Sales Letter

8. How to Write A Winning Sales Letter

Is There a Formula for Writing Copy?

If you read enough books on the topic, you are certain to find many formulas for writing direct mail.

AIDA

The formula seen most often is the same AIDA formula taught in many sales training courses — Attention, Interest, Desire, and Action.

In short, this simplified approach to direct-mail sales (adapted from face-to-face sales) calls for you to first gain your prospect's attention...then arouse his or her interest in the product or service...then create a desire for it in him or her...and finally call to action, in other words, close the sale.

There is nothing wrong with this formula, although it does not strictly apply to direct mail.

AIDA Formula

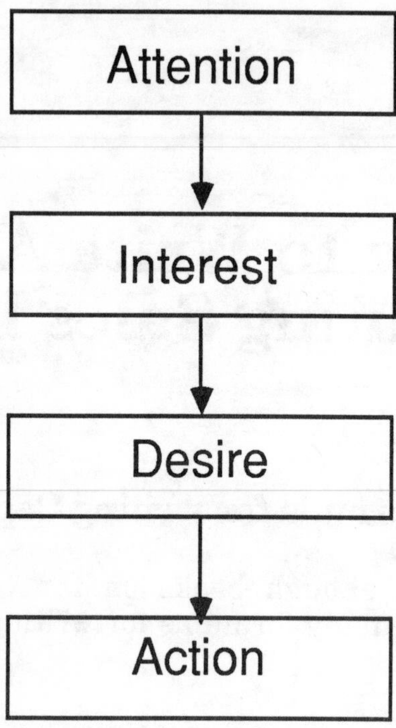

The AIDA formula is a simple one, adapted from conventional sales training. First you get attention, then arouse interest, then create desire, and finally call for action — ask for the order!

Stone's Seven-Step Formula

Bob Stone, in *Successful Direct Marketing Methods,* presents a more detailed seven-step formula suited for your direct-mail farm letters.

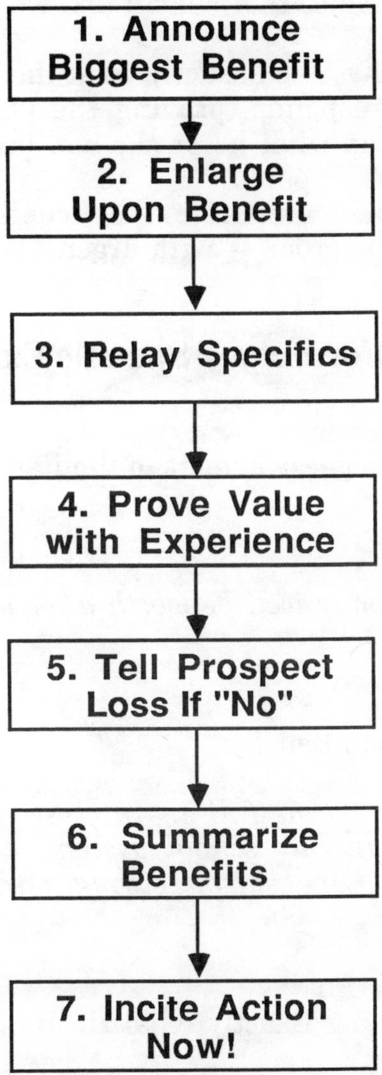

Stone's 7-Step Formula for direct mail is more precisely designed for mail order applications than the AIDA formula presented earlier.

You begin your letter by announcing — loudly and clearly — the biggest benefit to your reader. Then you move on to enhance that benefit and what it will do for them.

From there, you tell exactly what the reader will get if he or she responds (proving the value with past experience), and what he or she will lose out on if he or she does not respond.

Finally, you summarize the benefits again and then ask for the order — with urgency.

Seven-Step Formula — Specific Example

1. Announce Biggest Benefit to the Reader:

"Dear Neighbor,

Your home may well be worth a lot more than you think..."

2. Expand Upon Benefit:

"...with the recent fall in interest rates and the improvement in our school system, homes in our neighborhood have shown strong resale values of late..."

3. Tell the Reader Exactly What He or She Will Get:

"...by returning the enclosed card, you'll get a free Home Market Analysis. It will allow you to compare

your home with recent sales in our neighborhood..."

4. Prove Value with Past Experience:

"...dozens of your neighbors have already gotten their free Home Market Analyses. And it has helped them with some serious decisions about their homes..."

5. Tell Them What Happens If They Do Not Respond to Your Offer:

"...for most of us our home is our most valuable asset. And decision about it without full knowledge of the market can have devastating effects ..."

6. Summarize the Major Benefits:

"...your market analysis will not only let you know the current value of your home, but it will also help you decide on some serious questions about this most valuable asset..."

7. Incite Action Now!

"...to take advantage of this chance to find out about the hidden value of your home, simply fill out the card and return it by mail.

"I urge you to do this right away, since I'm only one person and many of your neighbors who haven't already taken me up on this offer are returning their cards now..."

Bob Stone's seven-step formula is quite good for using with your sales letter copy. Many of the country's leading direct-mail writers swear by it.

Do Not Let Formulas Bog You Down

While formulas are indeed helpful, do not get tied down by them. They tend to impede your creativity and communication.

In fact, many of the most successful sales letters of all time were structured nothing like either of the two formats above.

However, when you are first starting out, you may find them especially helpful to ensure that you cover everything and follow a logical path.

Remember, the bottom line is this: Direct mail is nothing more than salesmanship in print.

Write It, Read It, and Rewrite It

Just as with any form of writing, it is important to polish it up — and, of course, that means rewriting.

You may find it easiest to initially write as much as possible as fast as possible. Move briskly without slowing down to look words up in a dictionary or to try to come up with just that right word or phrase.

Then after you have completed a first draft, set it down and do something else. Later rewrite and polish it. And repeat the process if necessary.

Besides the obvious spelling and punctuation, you should ask yourself these eight questions as you read and reread your copy:

1. *Is the offer clearly presented?*
2. *Have I appealed to the reader in an emotional and personal manner?*
3. *Am I writing from the reader's point of view?*
4. *Are all the important elements covered?*
5. *Is it believable?*
6. *Have I distinguished the benefits from the features?*
7. *Does the copy flow, and is it written in a conversational tone?*
8. *Is it written using short words and easy-to-read sentences and paragraphs?*

Summary

This chapter covered some very important points in the area of writing sales letters. Initially it looked at two well-known formulas for writing direct mail — AIDA and Stone's Seven-Step Approach — and covered the latter in some depth with an illustrated example.

While formulas are helpful, do not let them bog you down. And always read and rewrite your direct-mail copy, keeping the eight questions posed at this end of this chapter in mind.

9. Starting Your Sales Letter

This chapter will go through step-by-step the first and most important part of your sales letter. If you cannot get the reader hooked from the very onset, then he or she will never read the rest of your letter.

Start out right, and the rest is easy.

The Headline

Like the headline on a newspaper or magazine article, the headline of your sales letter serves to call attention to your offer.

It is not mandatory by any means, but highly recommended.

In the formulas discussed in the last chapter, you wanted to either get attention or announce the main benefit of your offer. And what better way than through a bold headline.

The headline is the only part of your letter you may want to have typeset, but it is not necessary.

Get This Homeseller's Kit Absolutely FREE! Here's How . . .

Guide to Selling Your Home

Dear Neighbor,

Have you thought about selling your home?

If so, then you'll . . .

ABC Realty, Inc.

Get This Homeseller's Kit Absolutely Free —Here's How!

Guide to Selling Your Home

Dear Neighbor,

Have you thought about selling your home?

If so, then you'll . . .

Use a headline to gain attention or announce the main benefit of your letter. Typeset headlines (top example) make bolder statements, but typewritten headlines (bottom example) will work, too.

The headline is so important because if your prospect opens your letter, that is the first thing he or she will see; this is because you fold your letter so that it faces the reader when he or she opens the envelope.

And advertising research in direct mail and space advertising has proven its importance time and time again.

Direct-response ad expert John Caples says, "The success of an entire advertising campaign may stand or fall on what is said in the headline. . . ." (*Tested Advertising Methods,* p. 17)

Keys to Good Headlines

Good headlines should stop the reader and call attention to your copy. They serve as a messenger to get the reader to read your copy.

They should have emotional appeal, be interesting (or at least arouse the reader's curiosity), and offer something to the reader's self-interest.

Many good headlines offer news, and are even written in a "newsy" format — such as, *European Scientist Discovers Cure for Baldness.*

Questions often work well in headlines because they create immediate involvement. A classic example is the Max Sackheim-created ad for the Sherwin Cody School of English, which ran for over 40 years in various publications: *Do You Make These Mistakes in English?*

Examples of Winning Headlines

Here are some direct-mail headlines which have proven most successful over the years:

Will There Be BOOM and More INFLATION Ahead?
(The Kiplinger Letter)

"At 60 miles an hour the loudest noise in this new Rolls–Royce comes from the electric clock"
(Rolls-Royce)

Do you close the bathroom door even when you're the only one home?
(*Psychology Today* magazine)

Your Faith Can Move Mountains . . .
. . . Start with this one, please
(American Bible Society)

How To Win Friends and Influence People
(Book of the same title, Simon and Schuster)

Introducing! Big Savings up to 52% on L'eggs Slightly Imperfect Pantyhose
(L'eggs)

The Lazy Man's Way to Riches
(Joe Karbo)

If you are a careful driver you can save money on Car Insurance
(Liberty Mutual)

You are cordially invited to receive a free Executive Portfolio with your name stamped in gold prepared by the editors of Business Week
(*Business Week* magazine)

The Salutation

As simple as it may sound, the salutation is not always that simple.

The most common salutation in direct mail is the generic "Dear Noun" format, such as:

- Dear Friend
- Dear Neighbor
- Dear Professional

Qualifying Salutation

A qualifying salutation, which includes either an adjective in front of the generic noun or a descriptive noun, is best. Here are some examples:

- Dear Friend of KCET
- Dear Via Mesa Neighbor
- Dear Real Estate Professional
- Dear Fellow Lodge Brother

Though seemingly insignificant, this qualifying salutation tells the reader right off that you are either somehow related to him or her, or that at least this letter is targeted correctly.

If you, as a real estate salesperson, received a letter which started with "Dear Insurance Professional," then you would know right away to pitch it in the trash.

If the letter started with just "Dear Professional," then you would still be somewhat unsure it pertained to real estate.

However, if that letter saluted you with "Dear Real Estate Professional," then you would know that its contents were meant for you.

ABC Realty, Inc.

Dear Neighbor,

ABC Realty, Inc.

Dear Via Mesa Neighbor,

ABC Realty, Inc.

Dear Fellow Lodge Brother,

Qualifying your salutation helps let the reader know this message is for him or her, and adds credibility to you the writer. The top generic example says nothing; the middle example at least adds a geographic connection between the writer and the reader; and the bottom example (which would work well for a social farm) draws a strong connection between the reader and the writer.

Furthermore, in many cases the qualifying salutation helps draw a beneficial connection between the reader and writer, thus overcoming a major hurdle in any kind of sales — particularly in direct mail — and adding to the personality of the letter.

Open Salutation

Another popular, but not often advised, salutation is the open salutation.

ABC Realty, Inc.

Greetings!

ABC Realty, Inc.

Your home may be worth more than you think!

There are two other common ways to start letters, neither of which is advised. The Open Salutation (above) and the Shocker (below). Many successful mailings have used this latter approach, but only consider it if you have a dramatic appeal.

Examples of open salutations are:

- Greetings!
- Hi Neighbor!
- Hello From XYZ Realty!
- Good Day!

There is nothing wrong with "Greetings" on a handwritten note, but open salutations are less preferred for your sales letters since they lack personality when typed and mass-produced.

Moreover, they are, perhaps even subconsciously, unacceptable to the reader.

The Shocker

The famous Kiplinger Letter, which has run essentially unchanged for over 40 years, has no salutation. It starts off boldly with this shocker:

Will There Be BOOM and More INFLATION Ahead?

And then it moves directly to the dynamic sales copy.

A shocker, as its name would suggest, opens the sales letter directly — bypassing the salutation altogether — usually with some bold statement or question.

Popular with political fund-raising letters, this format cries for a very dramatic subject matter.

Something like this would not do:

Did You Know Your Neighbor Was Moving?

If you have a dramatic event, it might be worth a

try. Last year, a Coldwell Banker Realtor sent a well-done letter which started with this shocker.

Will the New Tax Law Hurt You as a Homeowner?

The offer was for a free Price-Waterhouse book on the new tax revisions, and the sales letter itself was very well done.

But remember that, at the time, the tax revisions of 1986 were big, big news.

Other Things About the Start of Your Sales Letter

Letterhead

Should you send your letter on your firm's letterhead? Not always.

While you will generally want to have the letterhead identify you as a real estate professional, some letterheads are not good for sales letters. For one thing, a busy letterhead or logo will compete with your message — particularly your headline.

For another, if your letterhead has several colors, it may end up costing you more than necessary to produce your mailings.

Sending a letter without a letterhead is probably not good either. You will lose credibility. Moreover, your broker may not like it, and if he or she is picking up part of the tab, that is especially important.

ABC Realty, Inc.

Serving all Your Real Estate Needs in Via Mesa for Over 15 Years

2200 Main Street, Via Mesa, AZ 80555

Dear Via Mesa Neighbor,

Dear Via Mesa Neighbor,

ABC Realty, Inc.

From the Desk of Jill Jones

Dear Fellow Lodge Brother,

Some letterheads,such as the top one, tend to compete with your sales letter, especially if you add a headline. Blank paper (middle) is not good either, since nowhere does it identify you as a real estate professional. Often it is best to make up your own simple letterhead like the bottom example.

The best idea might just be to make up your own simple letterhead like this:

ABC Realty, Inc.
From the Desk of Jill Jones

If you do make your own letterhead, keep the type simple, and not too bold. In addition, include the address and phone number at the bottom instead of the top.

Photos

The benefits of including your photo on mail-out materials to your farm have been well-documented in many real estate sales books. The photo helps to draw a connection between the mailing and any past or future face-to-face meetings you might have with your prospects.

However, if you choose to use a photo on your letterhead, keep it small so as not to dominate the page — and your intended message.

In addition, advertising research studies in direct mail have shown that placing potentially distracting items, such as photographs and board members' names (common in fund-raising mailings), on the left helps limit the message interruption these often present.

So, if you are going to use a photo — and there is no reason why you should not — keep it small, and place it in the upper left rather than the upper right or center.

When using a photo on your letterhead, avoid the distraction of having it too large (top) or on the right (middle). Ad research studies have shown that keeping such potential distractions to the left limits the way in which they compete with your immediate sales message. In addition, a format like the one on the bottom allows room for a headline on the right-hand side.

Dating Your Sales Letter

In most instances when you mail bulk rate, you will not want to date your sales letter. Depending on the quantity of other classes of mail, as well as other bulk-rate mailings, it may take up to 14 days for your letter to reach your reader, even if you mail locally.

While such a lengthy delay is uncommon, do not count on it *not* happening to you.

If you mail First Class, then dating is all right. But be aware, especially when you first start out, that delays in printing and mailing are not uncommon at all.

Say you planned to mail your mailing on Monday, the 15th. So a few days before, when you dropped your letter at the printer's, you used that date. Then at an open house over the weekend you got a solid offer, as well as another potential listing. Lo and behold, it is now Thursday, and you are still dealing with the counteroffers.

By the time you can get it in the mail (first class), it is Monday, the 22nd.

Now you have two choices: Reprint the letters, which will cost you money and add another two days' delay, or mail them as is and announce to your farm that you fell behind — and that perhaps they are not that important to you.

It is always safer to avoid dates.

This extends beyond a date in a heading. If you include a "limited-time offer" in your mailing, use more generic sayings, such as "for the next 30 days" or "for the first 15 homeowners."

Finally, if you really feel compelled to use a date, keep it more general like "May 1987" or "Spring 1987."

ABC Realty, Inc.

Dear Via Mesa Neighbor:

ABC Realty, Inc.

Dear Via Mesa Neighbor,

While not a big thing, the use of a colon after the salutation (above) gives your letter a more formal and less personal feel than a comma (bottom example). The little things add up to make your sales letters more readable — and more powerful!

Punctuation

Many of us have been taught in school to use a comma (,) for personal mail and a colon (:) for business mail. So it is assumed that, the minute you put a letter on business letterhead, a colon should be used.

Not true.

Always use a comma after the salutation when you are writing a personal sales letter to your farm, which will be most of the time.

It may not seem like a big deal, but it is the little things added together that make the big things work.

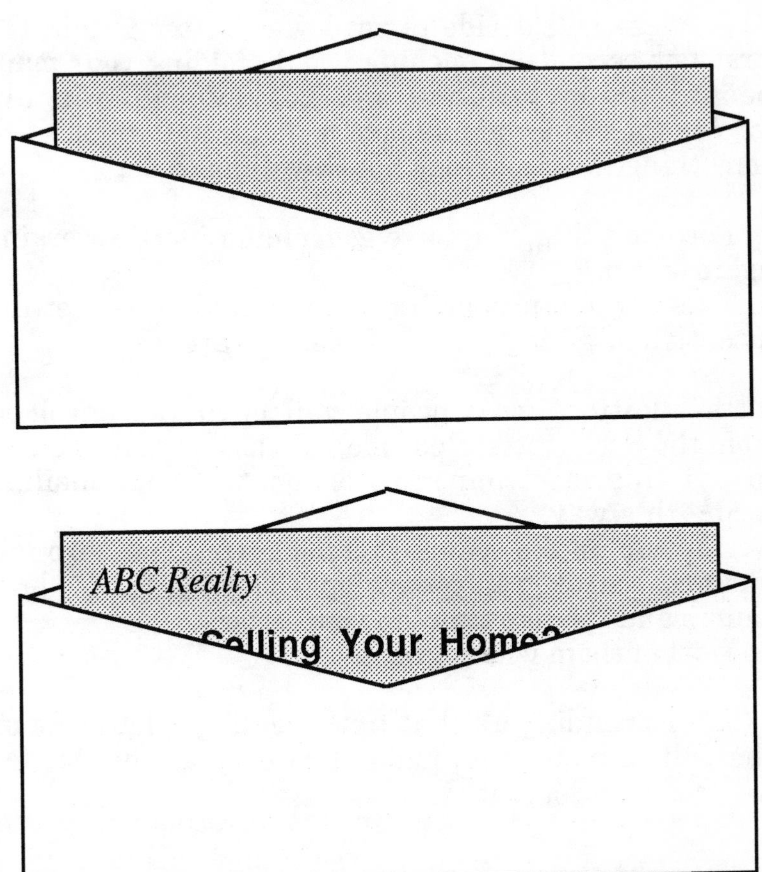

Always fold your sales letter so the copy faces out. Remember, the reader will decide within a second or two if he or she is going to read it. Anything you do to help will give you a better chance.

Folding and Positioning Your Letter

You were probably taught early on to fold letters

with the copy inside. This, however, is the exact opposite of what you should do when you mail your sales letters.

Readers will decide to read your letter within the first few seconds of opening it. By folding your main benefit-giving headline and copy inside, you are forcing the reader to pull out the letter and unfold it — something he or she may not be willing to do.

For one thing, you have got human inertia working against you.

The two main benefits of the headline — getting attention or giving a major benefit — are lost.

In addition, most people will open the envelope from the back (the sealed side). So it only makes sense to put this most imporant element of your mailing facing this way.

Do not make your prospects trudge through business cards, reply envelopes, return cards, brochures and the like to get to your letter.

Most of them will not do it.

After spending all that time creating a letter he or she will want to read, make it as easy as possible for the reader to get to it.

Personalized Letters

Personalized letters, which used to be pure luxury for direct-mail writers, have become a reality with the advent of the computer. Personalized letters are individually addressed to each prospect, usually using a computerized system.

Here are some things you should know about

personalized letters.

First, they will usually improve your response. And second, if you do them yourself or have them done by an outside service, they will cost you time and money. It is not at all uncommon to pay up to a dollar a page for the word processing on your personalized letters.

Since this will limit its application for most real estate farmers, this book will focus on preprinted letters.

But almost all of what it covers applies to personalized letters as well.

Summary

This chapter began a thorough examination of the farm sales letter.

It is without question the most important document you will enclose in your mailings to your farm. And it is what will make or break your direct-mail farming.

Much of the success of a letter depends on its headline. It should involve the reader, serve as a messenger and provide either strong emotional appeal or news of interest.

The next step, the salutation, proved not to be as simple as it would first appear. The salutation that in some way connects you to the reader or qualifies the reader is usually best.

For example, "Dear Fellow Lodge Brother."

There are two other types of salutations used; they are the open and the shocker salutation

Open salutations such as "Howdy!" are less personal, especially when typed on a page.

Shockers, which are nothing more than a headline used to open a letter, have been used for years by mail order companies, but they must be used wisely to be at all effective.

Finally, the chapter covered some of the basics of the start of a letter, including: letterhead considerations, use of a photo, dates, punctuation, placement of the letter into the envelope, and personalized letters.

10. Opening Your Sales Letter

In this chapter you will examine the most important paragraph in the body of your sales letter — the first one.

The Opening Paragraph

Used Without a Headline

When you *do not* use a headline, then the first paragraph of your body copy serves that purpose. Then your second paragraph becomes your "opening paragraph."

Used with a Headline

When you *do* use a headline (which is advised), then the paragraph right after the salutation is called the "opening paragraph" and is used — to borrow a phrase from the angler — to "set the hook."

Remember, the reader has gotten through your outer envelope, past your headline, and past your salutation. But he or she still has not decided to read your entire letter.

Now it's time to reel them in.

ABC Realty, Inc.

Now Might Be the Best Time in Quite Awhile to Sell Your Home!

Dear Via Mesa Neighbor,

Have you ever thought about selling your home?

ABC Realty, Inc.

Dear Via Mesa Neighbor,

Now might just be the best time in quite awhile to sell your home.

If you've ever thought about it at all, you'll want to hear this important news . . .

If you used a major headline, then the opening paragraph of body copy is designed to hook the reader and connect him or her with you. If you did not use a headline, then that is the first paragraph and your second works as an opening paragraph.

From the formulas presented before, you know you must expand on the benefit first presented and gain the reader's interest.

In addition, the opening paragraph needs to further qualify and connect you to your readers. And let them know the message upcoming is for them.

Example 1 — Consider this opening paragraph from a letter sent by Omaha Steaks International (a firm that sell steaks by mail order):

"I'm writing because I have reason to believe you are a person who appreciates exceptional food. If I'm right, you will be interested in this offer . . ."

Besides the superb use of the "you-and-me" style of writing, notice how this opening paragraph pulls readers into the copy by subtly yet clearly defining what is in it for them.

Example 2 — A similar example of the same idea came from a mailing sent out several years ago by the Franklin Mint:

"If you love and appreciate fine American furniture as I do, then what I'm about to tell you is truly exciting news . . ."

Again, the hook is set, and a meaningful qualification presented.

Example 3 — Here is a great opening paragraph from a classic space ad for Phoenix Mutual Life:

"This page is addressed to those thousands of earnest, hard-working men who want to take things easier some day."

Though slightly dated in its word usage, the message is again clear. Interest your readers and pull them into the copy.

Now contrast those opening paragraphs with this one in a letter actually sent out by a realtor (the name has been changed):

"I'm Doug Simmons, your local XZY Real Estate agent. We're here to serve all your real estate needs, from selling a home to managing rental properties."

The letter continued for eight more paragraphs, many of which read like Doug Simmons' biography. Unfortunately for Doug Simmons, no one was given a reason to read those other eight paragraphs.

No hook was set. No further qualification was made. And the letter failed.

Tips on Opening Paragraphs

Getting started with the main text of your letter can often be trying. Buzzing around in your mind are thoughts and ideas, but you need to lubricate the reader's path to get there.

Here are some useful tips on your opening paragraph:

"The Reason I'm Writing You Today . . ."

Used thousands of times by direct-mail writers, this opener, while not exciting, works. In addition, it puts you into the "you-and-me" style of copy — which may be reason enough to use it.

The variations on this are:

- *"I'm writing you today because . . ."*
- *"Let me explain why I'm writing you today . . ."*
- *"Because you are a homeowner in the Via Mesa area, I'm writing you . . ."*

This is a good format to have in your back pocket, but do not use it in every mailing to your farm.

"If" Starts

The beauty of starting your letter with the word "if" is that it has an automatic hook built in:

- *"If you're a homeowner in Via Mesa, then . . ."*
- *"If you're like dozens of your neighbors . . ."*
- *"If you, like me, think . . ."*
- *"Whether you're . . . " (variation)*

The negative variation of this can also work well:

- *"Even if you haven't thought about selling your home . . ."*

Many of the most famous direct-mail letters and ads of all time have begun with the word "if." If you do not try it, you may be missing out.

Dear Via Mesa Neighbor,

I'm writing you today to tell you about a special offer only for my neighbors here in Via Mesa.

Dear Via Mesa Neighbor,

If you're even thinking about selling your home, here are some interesting facts you'll want to consider.

Dear Via Mesa Neighbor,

As a homeowner in Via Mesa, I'm sure you'll want to hear about . . .

Three of the most popular ways to open a sales letter are with "I'm writing you today," (top), an "If" Start (middle), and an "As" Start (bottom). All of these are designed to both build a hook for the reader to read more, and help connect the reader with you the seller.

"As" Starts

Similar in many ways to the "if" start, "as" is not nearly as strong a hook, but serves as a very adequate qualifier.

- *"As a homeowner in Via Mesa . . ."*
- *"As dozens of your neighbors have already . . ."*

Two problems with "as" starts are: (1) they often come off a little cold and (2) they lead you away from a "you-and-me" copy style, since they put your letter into the third-person format.

Pose a Question

Questions, of course, are automatic hooks. But opening your letter with a question can be very dangerous. Why? Because if the reader answers no, then he or she not only has a good reason not to continue out of apathy, but not to continue because you said not to.

Take these two questions, for example:

1. *"Are you thinking about selling your home?"*
2. *"Have you ever thought about selling your home?"*

At first glance these appear to say the same thing, but the first one will get answered no by 99 percent of your prospects. The second one will get answered yes by 99 percent of your prospects — just about everyone has thought about selling his or her home.

ABC Realty, Inc.

Now Might Be the Best Time in Quite Awhile to Sell Your Home!

Dear Via Mesa Neighbor,

Are you thinking about selling your home?

ABC Realty, Inc.

Now Might Be the Best Time in Quite Awhile to Sell Your Home!

Dear Via Mesa Neighbor,

Have you ever thought about selling your home?

Questions are great ways to open a sales letter — but you need to be especially cautious with them. If your reader answers no to the question, then you have lost him or her for sure. Ninety-nine percent of your farm will probably answer no to the top question, while 99 percent will most likely answer yes to the bottom one.

"Have" and "how" are generally safer than "do" and "are" because they are more open-ended.

But carefully written, any question can work for you — and hastily written, any question can work against you.

- *"How can you say no to a free For Sale By Owner Kit?"*
- *"Do you want a free For Sale By Owner Kit?"*

In addition to getting a "no" response, questions can very easily evoke a big "Who cares?" from your readers.

- *"How much does XYZ Realty care about your home?"*

Questions can come off a bit abrupt in the opening of a sales letter. A way around this is to preface your question:

- *"Let me ask you . . . "*
- *"Just between you and me . . ."*

A final word about "no" responses: They are not always bad. If you have a very specialized offer, then you are actually doing your reader a favor by allowing him or her to accept or reject it in the opening paragraph. However, such specialized offers should not be sent out on a mass basis.

But in the case of the FSBO, the only people to whom you will be sending a letter are already selling their homes. And as such, posing what would be a "killer" question — such as, "Are you selling your home?" — might just work.

ABC Realty, Inc.

Now Might Be the Best Time in Quite Awhile to Sell Your Home!

Dear Via Mesa Neighbor,

A few of our neighbors and I got to talking the other day . . .

Do not overlook the story-telling introduction. You need only open and close with it — the rest can be pure persuasive sales talk.

Tell a Story

Story-telling in advertising, and in direct-response advertising in particular, has lost some of its luster of late — in the age of consumer skepticism.

But still everyone loves to read a good story, and most people like to tell one.

It is truly an art to be able to craft a story into a meaningful sales message. John Caples, who has been referenced several times in this book, wrote perhaps the most famous story-telling ad of all time, "They Laughed When I Sat Down to Play the Piano."

For an entire page he revealed how he had learned to play the piano by mail and eventually was able to amaze his friends with his new-found skill from a correspondence school (the advertiser, of course).

Only a professional advertising person could make this work, and even 90 percent of them could not.

However, as an introductory lead-in, such story-telling is not difficult to master. Take a look at these three possible introductions for your sales letters:

- *"Last week a couple of our neighbors and I were talking, and . . ."*
- *"Times have changed since we were kids . . ."*
- *"Six months ago nobody thought . . ."*

Good story-telling is the ultimate hook because if it is done correctly, people will want to read your sales letter just for the story element. And you need not continue the story throughout.

Instead, use it as an introduction and then tie it together in your closing.

Invitations

Invitation-type letters score high marks for qualifying and connecting you to your reader, but they leave you few chances for a true sales appeal later.

Types of offers that commonly use this format are fund-raising letters, credit card solicitations ("you have been preapproved to received a . . ."), and magazine subscriptions.

If you are inviting someone for an open house, then this format obviously makes sense. But for the bulk of your letters, it does not.

- *"You are cordially invited to view the home of . . ."* (okay)

ABC Realty, Inc.

There's a "For Sale" Sign up the Street — Come Take a Look!

Dear Via Mesa Neighbor,

You are cordially invited to view the home of . . .

You Are Cordially Invited to View the Home of

____

at

____

this

____

The traditional use of an invitation format does not lend itself to many farming applications. The most common, an open house, might be better suited to a true invitation card such as the one shown at the bottom.

- *"Here's a special invitation to join dozens of homeowners in your neighborhood as members of my newsletter subscription list . . ."* (not okay)

Many times in situations where you want to use an invitation as an opener, you will be better off with a printed invitation rather than adapting a letter.

Summary

There are indeed more types of openings than the ones presented here, but these are popular in direct mail.

This chapter covered in depth the first and most important paragraph of the body of your sales letter. You should also note that if you opt not to use a major headline, the first paragraph takes over for the missing headline, and the second paragraph becomes your "opener."

The openers presented here in this chapter were:

- *"I'm writing you today . . ."*
- *"If" and "as" starts*
- *Questions*
- *Stories*
- *Invitations*

Now, onto some helpful aids to writing the main body copy.

11. Tips on Keeping Your Letters Flowing

This chapter will cover many important concepts to keep in mind as you write your body copy. Since it is impossible to cover all the possibilities of body copy, this chapter will be devoted to overall thoughts and the subject of keeping your letters flowing.

The Transition Paragraph

The second paragraph of your letter is the "transition paragraph." Sometimes, of course, it simply expands on the first paragraph; in this case, it is really considered part of the opener.

The paragraph you want to be concerned with is the one in which you turn your reader's attention from interest to desire.

Consider this opening paragraph and transition paragraph in a letter you may have received in some form or another from American Express:

Opening

"Quite frankly, the American Express® Card is not for everyone. And not everyone who applies for Cardmembership is approved."

Transition

"However, because you will benefit from Cardmembership, I've enclosed a special invitation for you to apply for the . . ."

Or here is a more simple example from an insurance salesman:

Opening

"You need not be rich to need a financial plan."

Transition

"But with a complete financial plan from ABC Mutual, you may just have a better chance of ending up rich."

Like any rule, this "transition" concept can be broken.

This is particularly true of story-telling letters, which normally wind a long path before you take the reader into the offer.

Still no matter what format you use, turning the reader's attention is crucial to a good sales letter.

Copy Turners

A "copy turner" is a phrase or sentence that moves a reader's attention from the need, which you presented with your opening paragraph, to a desire for the product or service.

"That's Why"

Perhaps the simplest copy turner is "that's why." "That's why" works well with most openers.

Opener

"Like many of our neighbors here in Via Mesa, your home has probably gone up in value since you moved in."

Transition

"That's why you'll be interested in the Free Home Evaluation I'm giving this month."

"You, Too"

The phrase, "you, too," is not as universal as "that's why" because it needs to be set up with your opening.

Opener

". . . . Dozens of our neighbors have already picked up their Home-Protection Kits from me."

ABC Realty, Inc.

This Month, Get a FREE Home Evaluation

Dear Via Mesa Neighbor,

Like many of us here in Via Mesa, your home has probably gone up in value since you moved in. Knowing how much might just help you answer some serious financial and personal questions.

That's why you'll be interested in the Free Home Evaluations I'm giving all month long.

It's really quite simple . . .

Typically the second paragraph is used to "turn" the reader to your sales message. Transition phrases like "that's why" and "you, too" help smooth this path.

Transition

"You, too, can have the security of knowing your home is protected from outside intruders. And it's free just for the asking."

"You, too" appeals to a sense of belonging — "Well, if others are doing it, then why shouldn't I?"

Other Phrases That Turn Readers

The phrases above are just two examples of the

thousands possible. Here are some others you may want to keep handy for quick reference when you write your sales letters:

This is your chance to . . .

Here's what I'm offering you . . .

I'd like to offer you this:

Now you can solve this problem with . . .

In short, I've put together a kit . . .

You can have such an evaluation in a few short minutes . . .

Here's how you can eliminate those problems with a single phone call . . .

Here's your chance to find out just how much your home is worth today . . .

My offer is not for everybody:

Sales Without a Transition

Many sales letters move on to the sales message without a turning transition. Though this at times can be too abrupt, sometimes this abruptness works.

Opener

"Last month 11 homes in our neighborhood were broken into."

ABC Realty, Inc.

Here are some tips on protecting your home from outside intruders — and they're FREE!

Dear Via Mesa Neighbor,

Last month, 11 homes in our neighborhood were broken into — 11! I don't know about you, but I think that's scary.

With the help of the local sheriff's office, I've just put together a kit on how to protect your home. And I'd like to give you one.

Though transitions can help smooth the path, sometimes an abrupt paragraph change can add impact, especially if your offer is based on a dramatic preface such as the one above.

No Transition

"So with the help of the local sheriff's office, I've just put together a kit on how to protect your home. And I'd like to give you one."

This works best when your opening paragraph is dramatic, and your offer clearly solves the problem presented.

However, only unique situations call for this.

Body Copy Ideas

What you include in the text of your sales letter will vary tremendously upon your message. Here are some general tips on keeping that copy flowing and keeping it meaningful to your readers.

1. Simple Style

Although this was mentioned earlier, it bears repeating: Keep your copy simple.

That means simple, short words. Simple, short sentences. And simple, short paragraphs.

2. Use Present Tense

People want to know what is happening now. Not what happened last year, last week, or even yesterday.

"You feel a sense of security knowing your home is well protected."

3. Use Specifics

Compare these two sentences:

"Crime is on the rise."

"Last month 11 homes were broken into in our neighborhood.

Or these two:

"Home values are going up."

"The US Dept. of Housing announced last week that home prices increased 13% in the past 12 months — the biggest single-year increase in the last decade."

Specifics are much stronger.

4. *Avoid Slogans*

Slogans are used all the time in ads. And often they are worthless. A phrase like, "After all, we're the realtors who care," means nothing to your readers — even if it is strewn across your letterhead.

5. *Tell Them and Tell Them Again, but Don't Bore Them*

Good sales letters give a complete sales message, and this often means repeating benefits and covering all the possible benefits.

Do not be afraid to do this; but when you do, be careful not to bore your readers.

6. *Emotional Words Will Outsell Intellectual Words*

Intellectual words slow down the reader and impersonalize your message. Why use "beneficial in" when "good for" will do the job?

"Omitted" versus "left out" or "forgotten."

"Subsequent to" versus "since."

7. *Use Lots of Connecting Words and Phrases*

In school you were taught to write full paragraphs, with a beginning, middle, and end. That formula does not work well with the body of a sales letter. You do not want the reader to feel "complete" until he or she has come to the very end of your letter.

Short paragraphs help, as do connectors. Some examples of the latter are:

And — In addition — Also

And that's not all . . .

What's more,

What this means for you . . .

Most important . . .

In fact — In Short — In Brief

Why? — The result? — The answer?

If that's not enough . . .

I'm sure you'll agree . . .

And as I said . . .

Even if you don't . . .

Last but not least . . .

You get the idea.

8. *Bullets*

- Do not be afraid
- To use bullets
- To set off parts of your text.

9. *Numbering*

1. If you have more than a few unrelated points,
2. Using numbers will help the reader
3. Make transitions for you.

10. *One-Sentence Paragraphs*

Your high school composition teacher would not like it, but people will read one-sentence paragraphs more often than longer ones. The reason is that many people scan text before they read it. And if an important point strikes their eyes, they may stop to take a look at it.

One-sentence paragraphs work like subheads and are ideal to set off an important point:

"I'll personally deliver it to your home."

"It's yours free — with no obligation!"

11. *Visual Aids for Your Letter*

Making the words in the body of your letter easy to follow is not the only thing you can do to increase readership and response.

Visual appearance is almost as important.

- Use a large type face rather than the smaller elite. And avoid using standard computer printers for your output.

- Keep the margins wide and skip lines between paragraphs.

- Indent your paragraphs rather than starting them against the left copy edge. They are easier for the eye to follow this way.

- Sometimes you may want to indent an entire paragraph — make sure it is important.

- Use free-flowing punctuation — not just commas and periods!

- If you are using a word processor which can justify text (that is, make both the left and right margins the same, as is the case with most of this book), do not bother. The eye can more easily follow "ragged" right edges.

- <u>Underline</u> important words and phrases either with a typewriter or in pen.

- Do not be afraid to add some brief hand-written notes in the margin, or use check marks or exclamation points to highlight your copy. Just make them readable.

- At the bottom of a page that is to be turned over, write the words "over, please." Many people will not do it unless you ask them to.

ABC Realty, Inc.

Here are some tips on protecting your home from outside intruders — and they're FREE!

Making your letter visually appealing is important in getting people to read it. The example above has narrow margins, no indented paragraphs, it has justified text (right-hand margin is squared up), and no continuation at the bottom.

ABC Realty, Inc.

Here are some tips on protecting your home from outside intruders — and they're FREE!

(over, please)

This example is more appealing to the eye, and much more readable. It includes wide margins, indented paragraphs, "ragged" right edges (right-hand margin is not squared up), and broken-up blocks of copy.

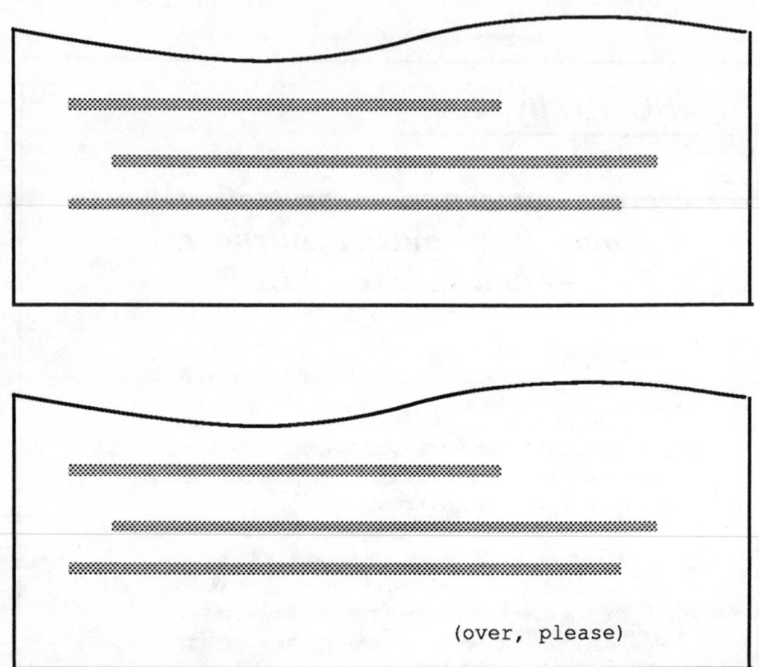

Though seemingly a minor point, the simple addition at the bottom of the words "(over, please)" makes sure the reader knows there is more to come. Without it, many will never turn the page.

Summary

In this chapter you looked at body copy, beginning with the transition paragraph — the one that moves your reader into the sales message.

Aids such as "that's why" and "you, too" can help ease the path for the reader.

There are times, however, when you do not want to use a transition. But it normally takes a very dramatic opener for this to be effective.

Here are some basic rules and guidelines for body copy:

- Simple words, sentences, and paragraphs
- Present tense usage
- Specifics versus generalizations
- No slogans (which are often meaningless)
- Tell them and retell them
- Emotional words
- Connecting words
- Bullets and numbers
- One-sentence paragraphs used as attention-getters or subheads
- Visual aids

Now it is time to move on to the close of your sales letter.

12. The Winning Close to Your Sales Letters

Just as with face-to-face sales, your farm letters need a good strong close. Before writing your close, remind yourself of the objective of your letter.

- A general face-to-face meeting
- A listing consultation
- An FSBO conversion

Keep this in mind as you write your final few paragraphs.

It is now time to close the sale.

Immediate Action

The biggest hurdle you must overcome in your sales argument is often not a "no" answer, but *no* answer at all.

With all good intentions, your prospect may read your letter, follow it to its logical conclusion, and 100% agree with you.

But unfortunately, with an improper close your prospect may take the reply card — with all intentions of sending it in — and tuck it away in a drawer, never to be found again.

This happens all the time in mail order sales. And such delays are fatal.

You overcome this problem by calling your prospects to immediate action. Compel them to do it now!

Offers That Expire

Dr. William Cohen presents three specific methods of overcoming this: limited-time offers, limited-quantity offers, and specials.

Here is a close from a letter sent by a mail order nursery. Notice how it calls for immediate action:

"But I must caution you. I have only a limited number of these exceptional tulips, and when they're gone I won't have any more for another year. I urge you to send your order in today."

Consider two these real estate examples:

"June is Home Protection Month here in Via Mesa, and I can only guarantee delivery of your Home-Protection Kit through the end of the month."

I only have a limited number of these For Sale By Owner Kits available, and "for sale" signs are popping up all over town.

Don't delay in ordering yours and miss out. Simply return the enclosed card, and I'll drop it by.

An immediate call to action is critical in mail order because often the biggest hurdle you have to overcome is not a "no" answer, but no answer at all.

"I only have a limited number of these For Sale By Owner Kits available, and "for sale" signs are popping up all over town."

These limited-time offers, whether stated or implied, help you close your letters and increase your response rate.

"While You're Thinking About It"

Another popular closing technique addresses the problem of people's natural tendency to put things off:

"Order your free Home-Protection Kit now — while you're thinking about it. And know that you're giving your family complete security — and yourself, peace of mind."

This one is not as strong, but much more believable; in other words, your readers can relate to putting things off. It is often used with very personal offers, such as fund-raising and insurance, but will fit well with several real estate farming examples like a home-protection or a fire-prevention kit.

Conclude Your Story

If you used a story as an opener, then your close can tie this sales pitch altogether and move the reader back to emotional elements of the story.

Here is the close to a fund-raising appeal for a childhood cancer institute. The appeal opened with a story of a little boy who was stricken with a very rare form of cancer. The story was especially emotional, since it was told from the eyes of his parents who had become supporters of the organization.

The writer brought back the emotion of the story with this close:

"Little Jimmy Miller lost his four-year battle with cancer. But you would have been proud of him up to the end — he never gave up.

"Now it's your turn to carry his strong-willed spirit and put an end to childhood cancer once and for all.

"Your caring gift in his memory will . . ."

Reemphasize Exclusivity

Perhaps less strong than limited-time offers, a reemphasis on the exclusive nature of your offer may help motivate your reader. In addition, you can always use it in combination with other closing techniques.

"This offer is only for Via Mesa homeowners like you and may not be transferred to anyone else.

"And I only have a limited number of them, so don't delay in returning the Reservation Card."

Phrases That Help You Close

Here is a handy reference guide to some words and phrases that may fit well into your closings:

Don't delay — Act now!

Why wait any longer?

Reserve your copy now, before they're all gone!

Order now while there's still time !

Do it today — Do it right now!

There's no time like right now to . . .

You need only pick up your phone . . .

I sincerely hope you'll join me . . .

It won't cost you a penny to mail the enclosed card today . . .

To take advantage of this free, limited-time offer, simply . . .

Go ahead, while you're thinking about it . . .

```
   This offer is only for homeowners like you here
in Via Mesa.  It may not be transferred to anyone
else.
   Don't delay in ordering yours and miss out.
Simply return the enclosed card and I'll drop
it by.
```

Reemphasizing the exclusive nature of an offer may not compel the reader to respond, but it may increase the perceived value of the offer as well as pave the way for limited-time appeal, too.

Reemphasize a Major Benefit

Just before or, ideally, during your close, you want to reemphasize the major benefit of your offer.

"You'll sleep just a little more soundly, knowing you've done all you can to protect your home. Don't delay — send in for your free Crime-Prevention Kit right now."

"I'm sure that knowing the value of your home is important to you. While you're thinking about it, why don't you drop the enclosed card in the mailbox for a Free Home Evaluation."

This serves to link the reader to the offer and puts him or her back into a more emotional frame of mind, thus more willing to accept it.

Tell Them How to Respond

It may be obvious to you, but it is not always obvious to your readers: You must tell the reader *step-by-step* what he or she needs to do to respond to your offer:

"To get your free Property Tax Update, simply drop the enclosed card in the mailbox. It costs you nothing, since I've already paid the postage.

"Or, if you like, pick up your phone and give me a call weekdays here at the office (888-1234) or evenings and weekends at home (888-9876)."

Do not assume that your readers will automatically respond just because you've inserted an order card into the envelope.

If you do, your mailbox will be empty more often than it needs to be.

> To get your free Property Tax Update, simply drop the enclosed card in the mailbox. It costs you nothing, since I've already paid the postage.
>
> Or, if you like, pick up your phone and give me a call weekdays here at the office (888-1234) or evenings and weekends at home (888-9876).

As obvious as it may sound, you need to tell your readers exactly what course of action they need to take in order to accept your offer.

Signing Your Letter

The signature area is also important, and your readers' eyes will scan for it on the page.

No one has proven that one complimentary close is truly any better than another. So simply using "Sincerely yours" is probably as good and as safe as any other.

"Sincerely yours" is preferred slightly over plain "Sincerely," but it is a personal preference only; it gets back to the "you-and-me" style of copy.

"Cordially yours" and "Cordially" are all right, but their common usage is waning.

There is nothing wrong with "Yours truly" if you are comfortable with it.

For some strange reason, many people feel the complimentary closing is a chance to make a last effort at being creative — and they often end up being trite.

"Your partner for all your real estate needs," not only sounds corny, but it takes away from the final sales pitch by distracting the reader's attention.

As to the actual signature, you should try to make it clear. People, you see, are often suspicious of illegible signatures.

Traditionally, direct-mail letters are signed with a first and last name. However, if you know a majority of your farm by their first names, then you can sign your letters with only a first name. But in most instances, this is not recommended.

Brief notes and follow-up correspondence are a different story. There a first name only is usually appropriate.

Your name and title just beneath your signature complete this area. There is not much to say about your name, other than to spell it right, but your title can have some twists.

Usually it is good to leave out the word "sales" (as in "salesperson") and "marketing" (as in "marketing representative").

If you are a member of the National Association of Realtors, then "Realtor" or "Realtor-Associate" is good. If not, then "Real Estate Agent" or "Real Estate Broker" makes sense.

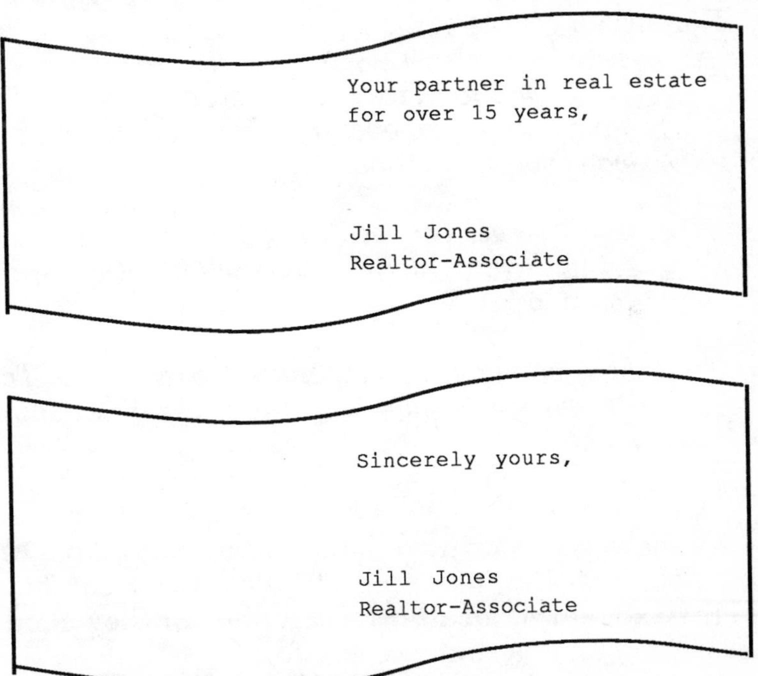

The complimentary close is your final personal message to the reader. Do not ruin it with a trite or cute saying. It will take away from your sales message at the most important closing seconds.

P. S. Don't Forget It!

If your prospects read nothing else on the last page of your sales letter, they will read the postscript, or P.S. Advertising studies have proven this for years.

So you want to make it count.

Many of the same ideas presented for the closing paragraphs apply to your P.S. — if not more so. Urgency, exclusivity, restated benefits, additional benefits, and special offers have all been used in good postscripts.

Here are a couple of samples:

> *"P.S. I urge you to place your reservation soon. We have only a few openings left, and I wouldn't want you to miss out."*
>
> *"P.S. Don't forget the wealth of information you'll get with your FREE Home-Seller's Kit. Order yours today!"*
>
> *"P.S. As a bonus gift I'll include a Free Home Tax Record Kit when you call to make an appointment."*

By the way, preprinted handwritten postscripts can be effective. But a couple of rules apply to them: (1) they should be neatly written and (2) they should not be very long (a sentence or two).

A preprinted handwritten P.S. will also look better if you have it printed in a second color, other than black.

```
                    Sincerely yours,



                    Jill Jones
                    Realtor-Associate
```

```
                    Sincerely yours,



                    Jill Jones
                    Realtor-Associate

P.S.  There are no hidden strings attached to
      this FREE offer.  Send for yours today
      before I run out.
```

The P.S. is a golden opportunity to add further impact to the closing of your sales letter. You can use it to restate benefits, add urgency, promote exclusivity, show new benefits not previously stated, or just about anything.

Furthermore, ad research studies show that people will scan the P.S. before anything else on its page, so you want to have a strong one.

Blue, for example, has been shown over the years to be the best second color to use on your sales letters.

And this applies to preprinted signatures, too.

You may consider having your printer print some of your letters without a postscript, and then you can add a special handwritten one to selected readers.

Whatever you do, never send a sales letter to your farm without including a postscript.

Summary

The last few paragraphs in your sales letter are critical. They close the sale.

Common themes included in the close are:

- Immediate Action (including limited-time offers and other specials)
- "While You're Thinking About It — Before You Forget . . ."
- Concluding a Story
- Reemphasizing Major Benefits

In this chapter you also went through several phrases which you can use at or near the close of a letter to help get your reader in the right frame of mind for a strong close.

Also, you need to very clearly tell the reader exactly how he or she should respond. Never leave such an important detail up to chance.

In addition, the chapter covered some tips on the signature, complimentary closing, and title area. Although these are small by themselves, it is the little things added together that make the big things work. *(Sound familiar?)*

Finally, you studied the critical importance of the P.S. (postscript). Many of your readers will read it first, or at least first on the page it is on — so make it count!

Part V

Mailing Your Mailings

13. Other Pieces In Your Mailing

Now that you have written your sales letter, you need to look at the other parts of your mailing — namely, the outer envelope, reply (or order) card, reply envelope, insert brochures, and possibly lift letter.

First, some general comments. The writing tips given previously for your sales letter apply to all the elements of your mailing.

Keep everything simple, benefit-driven, and written from the prospect's point of view.

The Outer Envelope

As mentioned in Chapter 6, the outer envelope is critical because this is what the prospect will see first. Most mailers use standard business-size envelopes, called "#10's" which measure approximately 4-1/4" high by 9-1/2" long. A standard 8-1/2" by 11" sheet of paper fits in a #10 envelope when the paper is folded into thirds.

Two other popular sizes are 6" by 9" (for which you fold your standard letter in half) and 9" by 12" (in which your insert material is sent flat).

It is also quite common, no matter what size envelope you use, to employ a "window" format. This is a small clear poly-covered opening through which the label appears.

The major benefit of the window format is that you can apply the label to the order card, which then shows through the window. This makes it easier for the prospect to return the order card since the name and address are already filled in for him or her, and it looks more professional and less like often unwanted "junk mail." In addition, you can code this piece to help you match the inquiry with the mailing.

There are several different schools of thought on the use of copy on outer envelopes: corner card only, teaser copy, and "official."

Corner Card Only

Obviously the safest route to take, this envelope has only your name and return address, typically in the upper left-hand corner of the front (or label) side.

The basis for this format stems from people's natural curiosity about what is inside. When sending a corner-card-only envelope by third-class mail, other steps should be taken to make the envelope look as much like first-class mail as possible. These include metering the postage and using a window envelope.

Rarely would you use anything other than a corner-card envelope for first class mail, because copy on the outer envelope indicates it is junk mail — and with first class mail you have paid a premium to avoid that look.

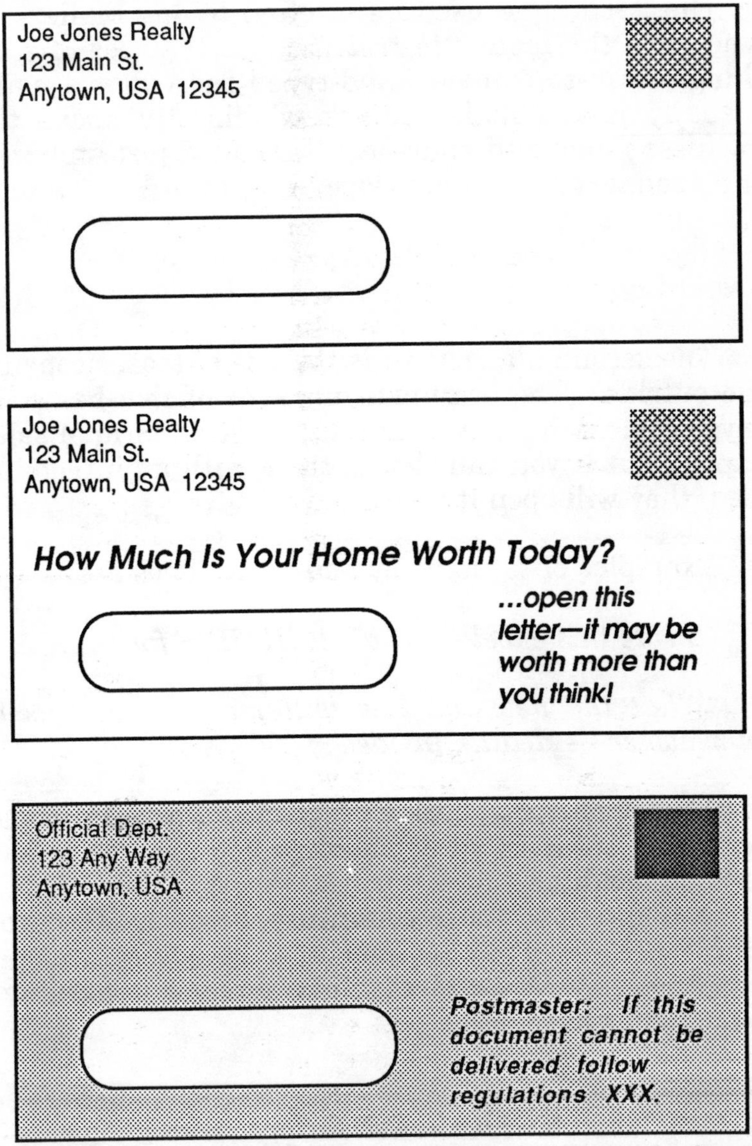

Joe Jones Realty
123 Main St.
Anytown, USA 12345
Joe Jones Realty
123 Main St.
Anytown, USA 12345
How Much Is Your Home Worth Today?
...open this letter—it may be worth more than you think!
Official Dept.
123 Any Way
Anytown, USA
Postmaster: If this document cannot be delivered follow regulations XXX.

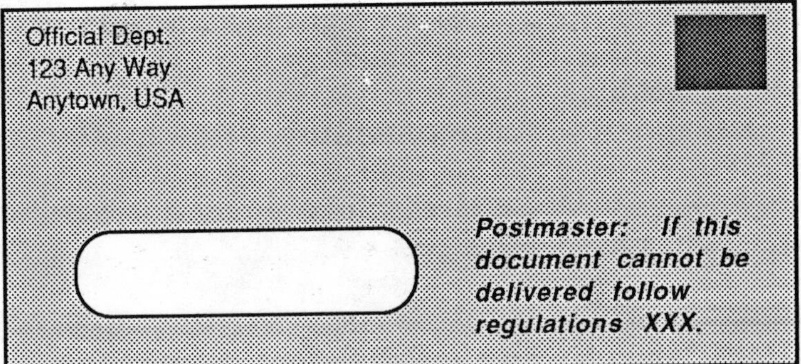

Three common formats for outer envelopes include the Corner Card (above), Teaser Copy (middle), and "Official" (bottom). Teaser copy can be very effective but is not as safe as the corner card. The "Official" envelope fools the reader into opening and can backfire.

One technique used quite often by big mailers — who have the money to test the effectiveness of such things — is to print a hand-typed individual's name (usually just a little bit askew) directly above the business name and address. This adds just an ounce of personality to your envelope.

Teaser Copy

The second alternative is the use of teaser copy on the outside. The argument in favor of this basically says people will know your letter is some form of sales appeal, but if you can "hook" them with an intriguing lead, they will open it anyway.

Examples of teaser-copy outer envelopes are:

"Inside this envelope is a FREE GIFT for you!"

"What the new tax law will mean to you as a homeowner — details inside."

Almost all the theories previously discussed about headlines apply to outer envelope copy, which serves as your headline.

In addition to those comments, be aware that you should not give away too much on the outer envelope. Give the readers just enough of a promise to get them to open the envelope.

"Official" or "Confidential" Envelope

A third school of thought on outer envelopes, one made very popular in the late 1960s and still employed today, is the "official" envelope.

These generally have words such as "Official Materials" or "Postmaster: If undeliverable, follow US Postal Code Section XXX.," and often have eagles imprinted on them.

The attempt is made to fool the reader into thinking he or she is receiving some sort of very important and official mail.

While this may get your letter opened, it is often a slap in the face when your reader discovers he or she has been fooled. And you lose credibility. You should shy away from these especially when you are doing a continuing mailing program, such as to a listing farm.

"Personal & Confidential" has been used on outer envelopes so often that it has become hackneyed. Again you are fooling the reader into opening your letter.

However, the words "personal" and "confidential" can be used in other ways on an outer envelope: "Your free confidential Home Review is just a phone call away."

One final word on outer envelope copy: Printing 300 to 500 custom envelopes for a particular mailing can be prohibitively expensive. This is another reason to send mostly corner-card envelopes.

Reply (or Order) Cards

There are two rules for writing the reply card: (1) restate the major benefit and your offer and (2) make it as simple as possible for the reader to reply.

You want to restate the offer because the reader will likely keep the card and discard the rest of your mailing. And this serves as a reminder of your offer and what it means to him or her.

You want to make it as simple as possible to respond in order to overcome human inertia, which always works against you in direct mail.

Not a rule, but also not a bad idea, is to add urgency to the reply device — "limited-time offer" or "don't delay in returning this card."

The back side of this order card can include your reply-mail information if you do not use a reply envelope. The latter, however, generally increases the response, especially if the offer is in any way personal; people usually will not send personal cards back without an envelope.

Brochures

Brochures can be just about anything separate from your sales letter which adds information about the offer.

☐ Yes! I'd like to find out how much my home is worth today. Please set me up for a Home Market Review!

The best time to reach me is __________

Preprinted label with respondent's name, etc.

This offer expires soon, so don't delay in returing this card.

Make sure your order cards are simple to fill out and restate the offer and major benefit. Also, it never hurts to add urgency to them.

Typically it might contain specific information about the tangible aspects of the offer — such as what a Home-Seller's Kit includes — and often has a photo or illustration if applicable.

You use it to reinforce the sales message and quite often restate many of the benefits covered in the letter — remember, "tell them, and tell them again."

You might also use a newsletter which contains recent listings and open houses, a company brochure, or (as noted earlier) a testimonial sheet from your past customers.

But the best brochures will be directly related to the offer presented in your sales letter.

Lift Letter

A fairly recent direct-mail concept, the lift letter, (or publisher's letter) is a brief note (usually printed on a smaller sheet of paper) which restates the offer, typically from a "higher authority's point of view."

> *Please read this note only if you've decided not to accept this valuable free offer!*

The Lift Letter plays on people's curiosity and the fact that most will not respond positively to the offer. Inside the offer is restated.

Most of them contain a handwritten note like this on the outside: *"Please read this note only if you have decided not to accept our offer."*

It plays on people's curiosity and the fact that even in a very successful mailing as many as 95% of the people will respond negatively.

While not common in real estate, agents have used a "broker's letter" to serve this purpose. And you may want to consider this, since the lift letter has worked in general direct mail for years.

Reply Envelope

You include a reply envelope to again make it as easy as possible for your prospect to accept your offer. This saves him or her the time of finding and writing out an envelope. And, if you include prepaid postage — using Business Reply Mail so you only pay for the ones you get back — you save your prospect the trouble of finding and paying for a stamp as well.

The business reply envelope makes it easier for your prospects to respond.

Rarely do you see a mailing without this element included.

Summary

This chapter covered the other elements needed to make your mailing complete and to ready it for printing and mailing.

It looked at outer envelopes, reply (order) cards, brochures, lift letters, and reply envelopes.

All the elements of a good mailing work together; so while these items are not as important as the sales letter, they still need to be done well in order to make a complete presentation.

14. Producing Your Mailing

Now that you have written your sales letter, the outer envelope, reply card, insert brochures, lift letter (possibly), and reply envelope, you need to get them produced.

Most of the services can be provided by your local printer, who often has word processing, typesetting, camera facilities, and art service in-house or has access to them.

If you have a small job, then there is no need to go elsewhere. But be advised that printers normally mark up such services since they, too, must make a profit for the service provided.

If you have a larger job and some time, then it is usually best to go directly to the service providers, such as typesetters, artists, and photographers.

Word Processing

There is no reason why you cannot type your own letters. However, if you have neither the time nor the desire, many outside services perform this for a very reasonable cost.

Since most of these services are schooled in secretarial-type letters, you may need to show them exactly what you want. If you have to, bring a sample direct-mail letter to illustrate the effect you want in your finished output.

Typesetting

Much of what you mail will be done on a typewriter, but for fliers and order cards you will want to consider typesetting.

Typesetting services can be found all over town, and while this is not a book on typography, it is good to know some of the basics so you can communicate with your typesetter.

Good typography helps readership. And, if your prospects have trouble reading your copy, then they will have trouble responding to your copy.

There are literally thousands of styles of type, most of which are very similar.

Some stylish typefaces, like Zaph Chancery (this one), are difficult to read and should be limited to special situations.

Of all the styles, most can be broken into two groups — serif and sanserif.

Serifs are the light lines and curls in the letters. This book, for example, is set in a serif face, as are most magazines and newspapers. Since people are more used to serif faces, they are preferred in most cases.

Moreover, it is these lines and strokes which help the eyes comprehend the words.

Here are some examples of serif type:

Bookman
New Century Schoolbook
Times Roman

Sanserif is type which does not have serifs (like this one). For large bodies of copy this style is harder to read.

But this style is fine for limited usage, such as captions beneath photos or illustrations.

Here are more examples of sanserif type:

Helvetica
Avant Garde
New Helvetica Narrow

Besides the styles of type, you may also use *italic*, **bold**, and ***bold italic*** type. These are harder to read for large blocks of copy but can be employed for important points, headlines, and subheads.

You also need to be familiar with the sizes of type. For body copy you will want to keep your type between 10- and 14-point. This book, for example, is set in 12-point type.

This is 9-point type.
This is 10-point type.
This is 12-point type.
This is 14-point type.
This is 18-point type.
This is 24-point type.

If the type is too big or too small, it is hard to read. One final note on type size — not all typefaces are exactly the same size, but they're pretty close.

YOU SHOULD ALSO AVOID THE USE OF ALL CAPITALS. These, as you can see, not only impede your reading, but tend to "shout" at your prospect. Nobody ever made a sale shouting at a prospect.

And finally, avoid large blocks of reverse copy (white type on a dark background); this is again more difficult to read.

It is what your words say, not what they look like, that will excite your prospects into accepting your offer. The harder it is to read, the less likely your prospect will read it. As advertising guru David Olgivy says, "You can't save souls in an empty church."

An alternative to typesetting can be found by using lettering machines. Kroy, for example, makes a machine which prints typeset-style letters on clear tape which you then apply to your artwork. If your office has such a machine, this will save you some money.

Desktop Publishing

One of the biggest buzz phrases in the personal computer industry is "desktop publishing." Open any newspaper or business periodical and you are likely to see an ad or article on the subject.

It is, in short, a method of producing near-typeset-quality documents on a personal computer, using a laser printer (somewhat like a photocopier) to output the finished product, such as an ad, flier, or brochure.

Small businesses (such as real estate firms) with a need for producing such quality collateral material are ideal candidates for these systems. They can cut artwork costs down to a fraction of what they are when using conventional typesetters, and can save you hours of time.

Apple Computer, with its Macintosh® and LaserWriter® printer, currently dominates this market, but IBM-compatible systems are being introduced all the time.

Small business experts predict that within the next 7 to 10 years, most real estate offices in the United States will have desktop publishing systems.

If you have one or have access to one now, your job of farming by mail will be a lot easier.

Camera and Art

For most of what you do, simple art is required. Generally a photo or two is all you will need. But if you do require extensive artwork, be prepared to pay for it. Artists and photographers are expensive, but fortunately there are ways around that.

One thing is to go through a local college or university art department. Many budding young artists are looking for ways to beef up their portfolios while making some cash on the side. This goes for photography students as well.

Clip art is another source of artwork your typesetter or printer may be able to connect you with. It is pre-done art work that is mass-produced and sold in volumes.

Real Estate Graphics (600 S. County Road, Suite

252, Minneapolis, MN 55426) is a company which specializes in this type of thing for real estate.

Photographs are also available for purchase from various sources, including photograph libraries, local newspapers, governmental agencies, and trade associations. Photograph libraries are the most expensive, as they are in business to serve large ad agencies who will pay a high price for the right picture. Newspapers and associations are less costly, and governmental agencies may provide photographs free of charge.

When you need to print a black-and-white photo, you must first convert it to a screened half-tone. Most of the time your printer will be able to do this for you at a nominal charge.

Color is another story. It must be "separated." This means the various primary colors are broken down for the printer. This is extremely expensive and all but prohibits the use of color in your mailings.

Printers

The commercial vendor you will most often work with is your local printer. For the size of print runs you will be doing, a small "quick" printer is your best bet. Several franchise operators exist in almost every town, such as Postal Instant Press, Sir Speedy, and The Big Red Q. In addition, there are independent small printers.

When you first start out farming by mail, check with several printers. This is important to do at the beginning, since it will behoove you to develop an ongoing relationship with a printer later on.

Get price quotes for a specific job — namely, your first mailing — and let the printer know you are planning regular, consistent printings of roughly the same size.

Sit down with the printer and talk about lead times required, services he or she offers, and ask to see samples of the company's work. And do not automatically assume the lowest-priced printer is your best bet. If you find someone with whom you can discuss all the aspects of printing, and he or she is reasonably priced, then you may have found your printer.

Ways to Save Money on Your Printing

There are many ways in which you can save money on your printing. Your printer will be able to help with them, but here are some ideas:

1. *Stick to Conventional Sizes and Formats.*

Most quick printers use standard sizes of paper — letter size (8-1/2" by 11"), legal size (8-1/2" by 14") and double letter size (11" by 17"). When you deviate from these sizes, it means your printer will have to waste paper, for which you pay.

This is not to say these are the only sizes you can use. For example, an order card is usually one third the size of a regular piece of paper; so if you stick to that size, he can print it "three-up" on an 8-1/2" by 11" sheet and then cut it into thirds for you.

2. *Colors of Ink.*

The more colors you print, the more your printing

will cost. Two colors, such as red and blue, cost more than black and a second color (i.e., red). And if you print two colors on both sides, it will cost more than printing two colors on one side and black-only on the other.

In most instances you will only be looking at black plus a second color, since your main type should be in black.

Second-color charges are high compared with the overall cost of a small run, but some printers "run" a particular color (other than black) on a specified day — i.e., blue on Monday, red on Tuesday, green on Wednesday. Often they will waive some of the normal fees if you run your second color that day.

Matched colors, in which you try to match a particular shade, will almost always cost more than using a standard second color.

3. *Paper*

Besides the size of your paper, color and weight can add to your printing costs. The most common types of paper used in a small print shop are 24-pound bond, 50-pound offset (or book), and 60-pound offset (or book). Your printer will have plenty of these in stock.

However, he or she will also offer a wide variety of types of paper, including glossy, textured, and colored paper. These all cost more.

If you are printing on both sides of the sheet, stick with the slightly heavier 60-pound paper since it will not show through as much and also has a better feel.

If you just print one side, then consider 24-pound bond or 50-pound offset. But compare their costs, as the feel does not change just because you are printing on only one side.

Textured stocks are rich looking, but get expensive in a hurry. That is why almost all the letters sent by large mail order firms are on 60-pound offset or similar stock. But in small quantities, expensive paper is not outrageous.

Black type on white paper is the easiest to read and is also the least expensive to print. If you choose to try a colored stock for your letter, keep it subtle, such as a light gray, buff, or ivory.

You should also avoid harsh colors for your brochures and order cards as they cheapen what you print.

4. Folding

If you have ever actually done a mass mailing using flat (unfolded) pieces, then you know the value of having your printer fold your materials. It is a lot of work to fold 300 to 500 pieces — and a lot more if you have two or three unfolded pieces going into 300 to 500 envelopes.

However, if you are using an outside service to do the actual inserting and preparation, it may offer this service, too. Compare the cost between the two before you automatically get your material folded by your printer.

In addition, if you are using a mail service, be sure to find out about its fold requirements. If they are using inserting machines (versus manual inserting) they will most likely need a fold-only edge — that is, an edge that does not have an unfolded flap on it. If this is the case, you need a "letter-fold" (copy out and headline up) versus a "Z-fold" (folded in the shape of the letter "Z").

5. *Rush Jobs*

Ninety percent of a printer's customers need to have their printing yesterday (and this same thing holds true for your other vendors as well).

Some rightly charge a premium for this, but in most cases the customer leaves saying, "Well, see what you can do."

Your printer will appreciate a comment like this when he or she asks when you need it done: "Well, what's your schedule look like?" or "I'm not in a big hurry. Standard service is fine."

And he or she will remember this when it comes time to return the favor — namely, when you really *do* need it ASAP.

The moral of this story: If you do not automatically ask for rush service, you will get it when you really need it.

How to Handle the Actual Mailing

Once you have your list prepared and mail pieces printed, you need to physically get them ready for delivery by the postal service.

You can either do this yourself or pay to have it done for you.

Doing It Yourself

Inserting, sealing, and preparing your mailing is a lot of work. This is especially true if you mail by third-class bulk-rate mail where you must sort it as well as fill out a form or two.

As a professional real estate agent or broker, you probably have several more constructive things you could be doing. However, if you wish to, carefully read the next chapter on US Postal Service requirements.

Getting Someone Else to Do It

Most real estate offices have limited nonselling staffs with which to operate. If you have someone, great. If not, then you will need an outside service.

Large commercial mailing houses usually have minimums of 5,000 to 10,000 pieces and are prohibitively expensive for small mailings of less than that.

There are mailing houses which cater to small mailers and you can look them up in the Yellow Pages; often, however, they are rather expensive.

Another source for such mailings is community service groups, particularly those serving the disabled. You might want to consider them because they generally do a very good job. Plus it may entitle you to special tax credits.

Properly supervised children can do mailings of this size, but you will want to keep a close eye on them. Smeared peanut butter and jelly on the bottom of your cover letter adds nothing to its sales pitch. Also, you still must tangle with the forms and affix postage.

When you work with any outside service, you will need to prepare a "dummy" mail piece. This a sample of the finished mailing in the exact order and direction in which you want the elements to be inserted. It is also a good idea to number the pieces so if they fall out of the sample envelope, they can be put back together.

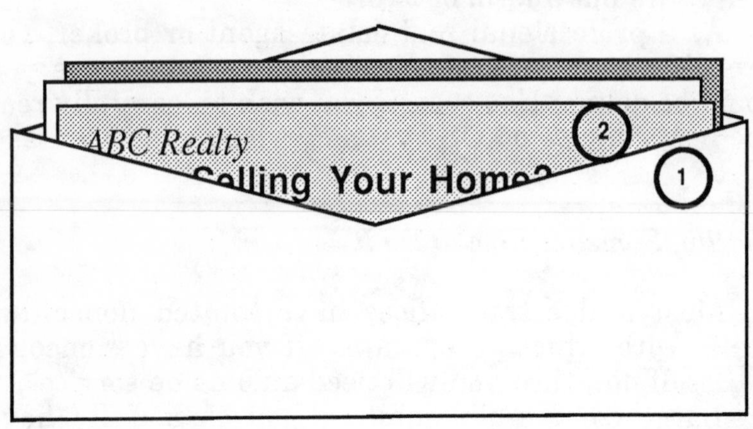

When you use an outside service to prepare your mailing, give them a "dummy" sample of the pieces in the exact order and position you want them. It is a good idea to number the pieces in case they fall out along the way.

Summary

This chapter looked at the various services and vendors needed to put out a mailing. At first this coordination will take some time. But once you do it a couple of times, it will move quite smoothly for you.

Those services might include:

- Word processing if you do not have in-house capabilities
- Typesetting which should be fairly minimal
- Camera and artwork services which are again not that often required
- Printer, with whom you will work quite a bit

As to the latter, there are many steps you can take to save yourself time and money on printing:

1. Using conventional sizes and formats
2. Colors of ink
3. Paper
4. Folding
5. Rush jobs

You also looked at some of the fundamental concepts regarding typography as well as a new topic, desktop publishing.

Finally, the chapter ended with a quick glance at how to prepare your mailing for delivery to the post office, the topic of the next chapter.

Recommended Reading:

The Copy-To-Press Handbook
Judy E. Pickens
John Wiley & Sons
New York, New York

Fundamentals of Copy & Layout
Albert C. Book and C. Dennis Schick
National Text Book Co.
Lincolnwood, Illinois

Graphic Arts Manual
Arno Press / Musarts Publishing Corp.
New York, New York

15. The United States Postal Service

There are two things you should know about the US Postal Service: (1) they have lots of rules and (2) they do not grant credit.

How to Save up to 54% on Your Postage

The US Postal Service offers four classes of domestic mail: first, second, thrid, and fourth.

First-Class Mail

First-class mail is the most prompt service available without paying additional fees for special delivery or Express Mail. There are certain weights and limits, but the cost for a single parcel weighing 1 ounce or less is currently 22¢.

Presorted First Class — A discount of 4¢ per piece on letter-type mailings (2¢ per piece on postcard-type mailings) is allowed for heavy mailers called "Presorted First Class." To obtain such a discount, your mailing must meet certain sorting guidelines (to 5-digit zip code), as well as contain a minimum of 500 pieces. In addition, there is an annual fee.

Carrier Route Presorted First Class — A discount of 5¢ per piece on letter-type mailings (3¢ per piece on postcard-type mailings) is allowed for heavy mailers called "Carrier Route Presorted First Class." To obtain such a discount, your mailing must again meet certain sorting guidelines (to individual carrier routes), as well as contain a minimum of 500 pieces. In addition, there is an annual fee.

Second-Class Mail

This is generally used by newspapers and magazines that mail at least four times a year. And it is not generally applicable to direct mailers.

Third-Class Mail

Referred to as "bulk mail" or "advertising mail," this class of service costs less and moves more slowly than first-class mail. It can include circulars, booklets, advertisements, and other printed matter, as well as parcels weighing less than 16 ounces. The standard discount rate for bulk mail is currently 12.5¢ per piece

Other requirements include:

- Payment of an annual fee
- 200-piece (or 50-lb.) minimum
- Zip-coding and presorting
- The words *Bulk Rate* (or *Blk. Rt.)*

Accompanyment of postal Form 3602 (Statement of Mailing Matter with Permit Imprint) or Form 3602-PC (Bulk-Rate Mailing Statement)

Five-Digit Zip Code Presort — An additional discount of 1.4¢ (to 10.1¢) per piece mailed is allowed if 200 or more pieces go to the same zip code — common in real estate farms.

Carrier Route Presort — An additional discount of 4.2¢ (to 8.3¢) per piece mailed is allowed if 200 or more pieces go to the same carrier route — possible in real estate farms.

Fourth-Class Mail

Also called "parcel post," this class of service is reserved for packages in excess of 1 pound (and books of any weight). Not generally applicable in real estate farming.

What This All Means

For your direct-mail farming, you have just two choices of service, first-class or third-class bulk-rate mail.

Even if you had a farm of 500 homes and were able to get a first-class presort discount, you would still pay 18¢ per peice versus 10.1¢ per piece for bulk rate — a savings of 43%!

Without presorting you will pay 22¢ for first class versus 12.5¢ for bulk mail — also a savings of 43%.

Furthermore, because the minimum to presort using bulk-rate only 200 pieces (versus 500 for First Class Presort), you are more likely able to get this discount on a bulk-rate mailing to a typical real estate farm, because they normally run between 200 and 500 homes.

That means by mailing bulk rate, you are likely to save 11.9¢ (22¢ regular first class versus 10.1¢ presorted bulk rate) per piece — a savings of 54%!

Think of that, you can save 54% on the cost of the single most expensive part of your mailing!

That is why third-class mail is so strongly recommended. You should use it as much as possible.

Doesn't Bulk Rate Mail Lower the Response?

The first response from most people is this: "Doesn't bulk mail hurt response?"

According to direct mail expert Bob Stone, "Third-class mail ordinarily pulls as well as first-class mail." (*Successful Direct Marketing Methods,* p. 219)

This is why almost all major direct mailers use third-class bulk-rate service.

In short, first class does not pay — at least not enough to pass up a 43% to 54% savings.

Payment of Bulk-Mail Postage

There are basically three ways to pay for your third-class mail: (1) permit imprint (or indicia), (2) meter imprint from a standard postage-metering machine, and (3) precancelled stamps. Special permits are required to use either an indicia or precancelled stamps. These are available from the bulk-mail department of your local post office.

Metering your bulk-mail postage will make it look very close to first-class mail, and it is easier to apply than stamps. However, a lot depends on how you prepare your mailings.

Precancelled stamps are effective but have more of a personal look rather than a business look.

The preprinted imprint looks something like this:

BULK RATE U.S. POSTAGE **PAID** POMONA, CA PERMIT No. 1

The permits vary in style, and wording must change depending on the type of service you are using (i.e., carrier route). And you can produce some indicias that look more like a metered imprint.

Address-Correction Services — Bulk Mail

You saw earlier how to use address-correction services to update your initial mailing list. Normally, after you have your list put together, you would not need to use this, since hopefully you will be on top of your farm movement. However, it never hurts to double-check.

To do this you include the endorsement "Address Correction Requested" on your bulk mail; it will normally be returned to you with the new address or reason for nondelivery. When mailing third class, the single-piece rate will be charged with each returned piece.

In addition, you can use the more complete endorsement, "Do Not Forward, Address Correction Requested, Return Postage Guaranteed." Some post offices prefer this latter endorsement.

The bulk-mail department of your post office can provide you with complete information.

Business Reply Mail

One of the best services provided by the post office for the direct-mail farmer is Business Reply Mail.

Business Reply Mail lets you furnish a postage-paid return envelope (or card) to your prospect and only pay for the ones you receive back.

There are specific printing regulations for the reply card or envelope and it requires an annual permit.

The per-piece fee can be paid through an account (called a Business Reply Account) set up with the post office or directly with each piece. That fee is 7¢ each with a Business Reply Account and 23¢ each without an account. However, there is an additional annual fee for the account so it is designed for high-volume users.

Summary

This chapter covered the basics of the United States Postal Service.

It began by looking at a cost comparison between first-class and bulk-rate mail.

For most direct-mail real estate sales letters, bulk

mail is more than adequate and will save you between 43% and 54% on the most expensive single item in your mailing.

Despite rumors to the contrary, response rates from bulk rate and first class do not vary considerably.

You can pay your third-class postage with either precancelled stamps, metering, or preprinted imprints. Stamps and metered imprints look more like first class (which is generally good), but depending on who prepares your mailing, you may want to use an indicia.

Business Reply Mail was also covered in this chapter.

One last note: At most medium to large post offices, there is a particular person in charge of all the bulk mail. This person is good to get to know as he or she can answer a lot of questions for you and explain the sometimes-complicated rules.

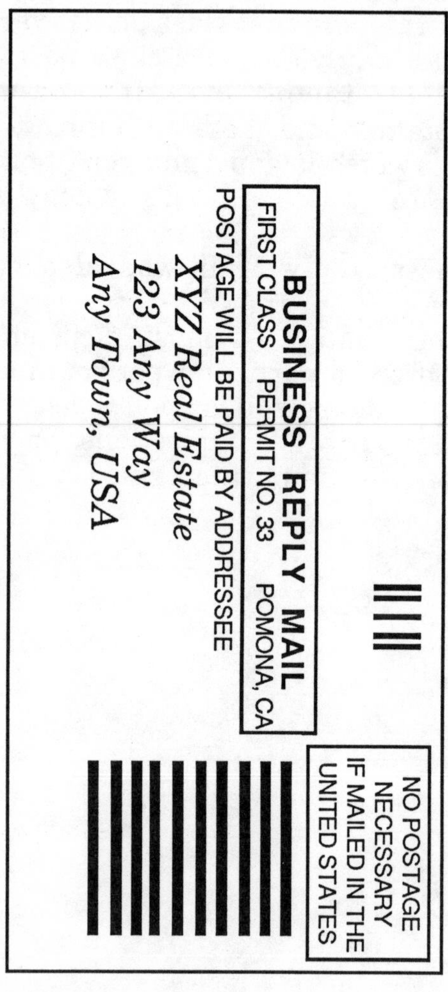

Sample Business Reply Envelope

16. Wrapping Things Up

This text has covered everything from sizing your farm to farm sales letters to postal requirements.

Once again, it is important to recall how all of your farm efforts — personal contact, phone calls, and direct mail — must work together.

Other Ways to Mail to Your Farm

You looked at both newsletters and farm sales letters, but there are other times when you will want to mail to your farm.

Personal Notes

Keeping on top of your farm means knowing what is going on with its residents. Many times you will read or hear about a special event such as a birth, a work promotion, or a marriage. These are ideal times to drop a quick note, usually handwritten, to say congratulations, etc.

They do not need to be long or extensive, but they

should be timely. It is best to stock up on some cards and have them in your desk drawer.

One good source for such cards particularly designed for real estate is Harrison Publishing Co. (624 Patton Avenue, Ashville, NC 28806). They have all sorts of handy, good-looking cards for a lot of needs at very reasonable prices. (You can write the firm or call them toll-free at 1-800-438-5829 for a free brochure and sample cards.)

Thank-You Cards

Every time you make a personal visit or even a long phone call, it is a good idea to drop a brief thank-you note in the mail.

This is not always practical, but farming is, after all, a lot of work. And you only get out what you put in.

Thank-you notes and other cards help you keep continuing contact with your farm.

Co-Op Mailings

In most areas there are firms which put together co-op mailings to residents. Such mailings usually include coupons from local restaurants and shops, and offers from service-related businesses like insurance agencies and eye care centers.

The cost of these mailings can be very low since all the participants share the postage, printing, and production costs.

Most will not align with an individual agent's farm but may work well for the brokerage office. One caution: There has been significant fraud in this industry in the area of mailers saying they are sending 10,000 packets and they only send 2,000. A couple of things will help: (1) never prepay for one of these co-ops and (2) require that the firm attach the USPS Form 3602 (Bulk-Mailing Statement) with your invoice. Firms that will not go along with such requests are probably not worth doing business with.

Testing and Your Mailings

Each time you do a mailing, you will want to track both its costs and return.

To keep track of the costs, use the attached budget worksheet. To track your response data, you should employ a system used by direct-mail firms for decades — "key coding."

Key coding is the method of coding your response device so that you can trace its source. Typically you just type a small code somewhere on the reply piece.

In addition to the source code, you will want to keep a master logbook of offers you sent.

Farm Mailing Budget Worksheet

Printing/Graphics Costs	**GRAPHICS**	**PRINTING**
Cover Letter	______	______
Insert Piece #1	______	______
Insert Piece #2	______	______
Order Card	______	______
Outer Envelope	______	______
Reply Envelope	______	______
Total Printing	______	______

Mailing Costs

Inserting/Prep. ______________

Postage ______________

Premium

Front-End Premium______________ ______________

Back-End Premium______________ ______________

Other — Misc.

______________________ ______________

Total Cost for Mailing ______________

☐ Yes! I'd like tc find out how much my home is worth today. Please set me up for a Home Market Review!
The best time to reach me is ________

Preprinted label with respondent's name, etc.

This offer expires soon, so don't delay in returing this card.

FM-6/87

Tracking response and tying costs with return is the crux of mail order and farming by mail. The key code on the reply device helps you keep track of what offers are working.

Low Response

When you send out a farm sales letter, do not get braced for scores of cards to flood your desk. Depending on your offer, 2% response is good and 5% response is outstanding.

Two percent of 500 homes is only 10 cards.

But remember, it only takes a few leads to make your whole farm mailing program work. Additionally, you still have the PR benefit of getting your name in front of your prospects even if they do not respond.

Testing

If you have read other books on direct mail, then you are probably familiar with testing. It is, for mass mailers, the backbone of the industry.

In a small farm environment it is hard to conduct such testing because one or two random responses can throw the entire test off. However, you do want to keep track of which offers generate the most leads, and don't be afraid to repeat them often.

You may get tired of mailing the same package to your farm every third month but that is because you spend a lot of time with it. Your readers, on the other hand, may not have even noticed it before.

People's interests change quite rapidly. As David Ogilvy says, "You are not mailing to a standing army, but rather a marching parade."

Following Up Your Leads

Direct-mail leads should be top priority since they are "hot."

If someone in your farm took the time to read through what may have been a lengthy offer and then returned your reply card, make certain you get back to your prospect quickly, before he or she loses interest.

Final Comments on Farming

Farms take time to get established. Just as the agricultural farmer plants his seeds in the spring and harvests his crops in the fall, so to othe real estate farmer must be patient and work hard.

Sometimes it is a trying experience, but as proven by thousands of real estate professionals nationwide, the long-term rewards are well worth it.

References

Chapter 3

Page 30 — Direct Marketing, Garden City, N.Y., February 1987.

Chapter 7

Page 81 — John Caples, *Tested Advertising Methods,* 2nd ed., Reward Books/Prentice Hall, Inc., Englewood Cliffs, N.J., 1974, p. 15.

Page 83 — William Cohen, *Building A Mail Order Business,* 2nd ed., John Wiley & Sons, New York, N.Y., 1985, p. 96.

Pages 83-85 — Herschell Gordon Lewis, *Direct mail copy that sells!* Prentice Hall, Inc., Englewood Cliffs, N.J., pp. 15-16.

Page 86 — Bob Stone, *Successful Direct Marketing Methods,* 2nd ed., Crain Books (imprint by National Textbook Co., 4255 W. Touhy, Lincolnwood, Ill., 60646), 1979, p. 33.

Chapter 8

Pages 104-108 — Bob Stone, op. cit., pp. 210-212.

Chapter 9

Page 113 — John Caples, op. cit., p. 17.

Chapter 12

Page 160 — William Cohen, op. cit., pp. 113-114.

Chapter 15

Page 202 — Bob Stone, op. cit., p. 219.

Appendix

Sample Farm Letters

ABC Realty

Your home may be worth a lot more than you think . . .

Dear Via Mesa Neighbor,

Now may be the best time in a long while to tap the hidden value of your current home and move into the home you've always dreamed of.

That's because your current home may be worth a lot more than you think. And knowing this value may help you answer some serious questions facing many homeowners today.

Just last month a house in our neighborhood sold for 50% more than the owners thought they could possibly get. And with funds they received from that sale, they were able to get into their dream house!

With falling interest rates and the recent improvement in our local school system, your home, too, has probably appreciated quite a bit.

That's why I'm offering a FREE Home Evaluation to homeowners like you here in Via Mesa.

> With this evaluation you'll get a complete written analysis of the value of your home based on recent sales of comparable homes in the neighborhood.

Five years ago -- the last time the real estate market was this strong -- many homeowners were caught off guard. And they missed an ideal opportunity to sell because they didn't know how much their own homes were worth.

(over, please)

You, too, may be missing out on the hidden value of your home if you don't at least find out its current value.

Remember, there's absolutely no obligation with my offer!

You get your Free Home Evaluation and I say good-bye -- and let you decide what it may mean to you.

To take me up on this offer, all you have to do is return the enclosed postage-free card by mail. But I urge you to do it today, since this offer is good only through the end of the month.

Sincerely yours,

Jill Jones
Realtor-Associate

P.S. In a hurry? Give me a call either during the day here at the office (987-9876) or evenings and weekends at home (987-6789).

ABC Realty

Fire season is here —
Is your home fully protected?

Dear Via Mesa Neighbor,

Like most of us, Doug and Susan Johnson thought their home was safe from the dangers of fire. Then, on a hot July afternoon two years ago, a fiery blaze ripped through their home, leaving nothing but ashes and a bare foundation.

The Johnsons were lucky, since they were both at work and their four-year-old son, Jason, was at pre-school. No one was hurt, but their house was completely destroyed.

"That fire could have been prevented," Doug says today. "If I had just taken a few simple steps, it never would have happened."

How safe is your home?

If you're like most of us, fire-prevention is often one of the last things you think about.

But as that July afternoon announced to all of us, it shouldn't be.

That's why, in cooperation with the Via Mesa Fire Dept., I've put together a Fire-Protection Kit designed to help you protect your home.

<u>And it's absolutely free for the asking</u>!

Your Fire-Protection Kit includes . . .

(over, please)

* A 24-page booklet entitled, "40 Ways To Protect Your Home,"

* A handy directory of emergency phone numbers you can keep by your phone,and

* A 25%-off discount coupon from Fred's Hardware on a home fire extinguisher and smoke detector.

It's easy to put things like this off. Few of us like to think about such tragedies.

But don't let what happened to Doug and Susan Johnson -- or something even worse -- happen to you.

Right now, while you're thinking about it, take the return postcard and drop it in the mail. I will personally deliver your Fire-Protection Kit as soon as I get your card.

Sincerely yours,

Jill Jones
Realtor-Associate

P.S. July has been designated "Fire Prevention Month" here in Via Mesa. And I can only guarantee delivery of your FREE kit through the end of the month. So order yours today!

ABC Realty

Will the new tax law hurt you as a homeowner?

Dear Via Mesa Neighbor,

According to a recent article in the Wall Street Journal, more than 75% of us pay more taxes than we legally have to.

And with the confusion surrounding the new tax law -- especially as it applies to homeowners -- that figure is sure to go up in 1988.

Together with Smith & Smith CPAs, our firm has put together a valuable booklet on what the new tax law means to homeowners here in Via Mesa.

Called the "Homeowner's Survival Guide to the New Tax Law," this easy-to-follow 16-page booklet tells you exactly what effect these changes have on us -- as well as money-saving ideas for homeowners like you.

I'm sure you'd like to save money on your taxes, and this booklet will get you off to a good start.

To get your free booklet, simply drop the enclosed card in the mail. There's no catch.

Sincerely yours,

Jill Jones
Realtor-Associate

P.S. Return this card right now while you're thinking about it. Tax time isn't far away.

Index